W9-AQC-850

LIBER
HISTORIAE FRANCORUM

Edited and translated with an Introduction

by
Bernard S. Bachrach

Coronado Press   1973

Published by
Coronado Press
Box 3232
Lawrence, Kansas 66044

SBN 87291—058—X

Manufactured in the USA

η-5-78

For my sons Jamie, David, and Daniel

Contents

Errata

Page 115. Line 6: "Alanos d" should read "Alanos de"
Page 115. Line 11: "non iugiter" should read "nos iugiter"
Page 120. "Childebert III, Merovingian King" should read "Childeric I, Merovingian King"
[Page 125]. Genealogy chart: "Theudebert III" should read "Theuderic III"

Introduction*

Three early medieval narrative histories — Gregory of Tours' *History of the Franks,* Fredegar's *Chronicle* (with its continuations), and the anonymous *Liber Historiae Francorum (LHF)* — provide modern scholars with the basic outlines of "what happened" in Merovingian Gaul. Gregory's history and the most important parts of Fredegar's narrative are available in English translation so that college students studying medieval history have easy access to these basic materials. The *LHF,* on the other hand, appears here for the first time in English translation, and for the first time in its entirety in any modern language.

The present volume makes available our best source for the history of Merovingian Gaul during the seventh century. In addition, the *LHF* illustrates the ideas, biases, and historiographical methods of its author — a man who was well-educated by the standards of his time in Gaul and a man who, for a while at least, was close to the center of political power in Neustria. In these hectic times the Merovingian kings, or at least most of them, were *rois fainéants* and the important families in northern Gaul (Neustria and Austrasia) struggled to exercise real power. Intellectual life in Gaul had probably reached its nadir. Religious enthusiasm was less

- 9 -

than conspicuous. The author of the *LHF*, moreover, not only chronicles his own perceptions of declining royal power and contemporary morality but imposes his views upon the past when he writes about the early history of the Frankish people and the society of Merovingian Gaul in the age following the disappearance of Roman rule.

Scholars agree that our author has a clear Neustrian bias. Thus he concentrates on Neustrian monarchs, clerics, and politics while giving meagre attention to what was happening in Austrasia, Burgundy, and Aquitaine. He refers to Neustria as Francia and he calls its inhabitants Franks rather than Neustrians. The inhabitants of Austrasia, however, a people who in an ethnic sense may well merit being called Franks, are described as either Austrasians or Ripuarians.

A significant example of this bias can be seen in his treatment of the Neustrian queen Fredegund whose capacity for brutality and trouble-making were widely known through the Merovingian era and condemned by contemporary and later commentators. From the *LHF* we obtain a picture which is less critical than that of the Fredegund which emerges from, for example, the *History* written by Gregory of Tours. The defense of Fredegund which we find in the *LHF* is, by the standards of Merovingian historiography, relatively subtle. Our author accomplishes this, in part, by describing Fredegund's talents. She is credited with contriving the plan and suggesting the use of camouflage which resulted in the victory of a numerically inferior Neustrian army over a larger invading force from Austrasia and Burgundy. Her capacity for motherly compassion is also emphasized as is the fact that she received an honorable Christian burial in the church of Saint Vincent.

In addition to balancing Fredegund's talents and virtues against her well-known acts of deceit and brutality, our author takes pains to omit many of the evil doings which other historians attribute to her. Even more effective than trying to present a balanced picture of Fredegund is our author's technique of comparing and contrasting her acts with those of her arch-enemy, Queen Brunhild. In the *LHF*, Brunhild is blamed for many atrocities for which she was probably not responsible, including the murders of her grandson, Theuderic II, and of her great-grandsons, Theuderic's children. Our author also condemned Brunhild for her uncanonical marriage to her nephew Merovech. Her horrible death by torture is pictured by our author as an end which she justly deserved. The description of the burning of her corpse and the scattering of her ashes are meant to impress the reader with the extent of Brunhild's evil. When Brunhild's horrible demise is compared with Fredegund's honorable repose at the church of Saint Vincent, the reader cannot easily avoid the conclusion that the Neustrian queen, regardless of all the evil she had done, is to be preferred over her Austrasian rival.

Our author's account of events and places in the Paris region, the very heart of Neustria, has suggested to scholars that he was a native of this *civitas*. Particular attention is paid in the *LHF* to the monasteries of Saint Vincent (today Saint-Germain des Près) and Saint Denis. For example, our author tells us of the foundation of the monastery of Saint Vincent by King Childebert I. We also learn that Childebert was buried there as was Queen Fredegund and Bishop Germanus of Paris. Our author is at least equally interested in and knowledgeable about the monastery of Saint Denis. He panegyrizes King Dagobert I, who founded the monastery of Saint Denis, and relates a story, unique at the time, about the desecration of the saint's relics. It seems that King Clovis II, Dagobert's son, was very impressed by what he believed to be Saint Denis' power; thus the King desired some of the holy man's corpse for his personal relic collection. As the story goes, Clovis cut off one of the arms from the corpse at the instigation of the devil. Understandably, Clovis' act was not appreciated by the monks, and our author condemns him vigorously: "Clovis, having been instigated by the devil, cut off the arm of the blessed martyr Denis. At the same time he brought ruin to the kingdom of the Franks with disastrous calamities. This Clovis, moreover, had every filthy habit. He was a seducer and a debaser of women, a glutton, and a drunk."

It is very likely that our author spent some time at both the monastery of Saint Denis and that of Saint Vincent. When he wrote the *LHF*, our author was living some place north of the Seine river and thus could not have been residing at the monastery of Saint Vincent, since it is located south of the Seine. The monastery of Saint Denis, however, is situated north of the Seine, and scholars generally agree that he was there when he wrote the *LHF* in 727.

Although we will probably never be able to ascertain the identity of the man who wrote the *LHF*, we can, as we have seen above, learn a great deal about him from his work. For example, our author provides a much greater degree of detail about the political activities in and about the court of King Theuderic III (673-690) than about any other monarch during the later seventh and early eighth centuries. Among other things we learn about Theuderic that we do not learn about most of his royal contemporaries are the names of his sons, of his wife, of his mother and father, and of his brothers. We also learn about the political intrigues affecting Theuderic's court and the struggles of the magnates for the very important office of mayor of the palace.

When Theuderic succeeded his older brother Chlotar III as King of Neustria in 673, Ebroin was mayor of the palace. Shortly thereafter, however, Theuderic was temporarily deposed as the result of a conspiracy aimed essentially at Ebroin. A new conspiracy was initiated against Theuderic's successor, King Childeric II, and our author maintains with an air of certainty concerning the leaders, "Ingobert to be sure, Amalbert, and other Frankish magnates stirred up an insurrection against Childeric." Further, we learn that this plot was supported by Bishop Leudegar of Lyons and his brother Gaerin, and finally that Childeric was murdered by a Frank (Neustrian) named Bodilo.

With the success of this conspiracy, Leudesius became mayor of the palace and Theuderic regained the throne. After a short time, however, another plot was initiated, this time by Ebroin, who had been driven from the mayorship a few years earlier. We learn that Ebroin moved against Leudesius and Theuderic from his place of exile at the monastery of Luxeuil in Burgundy. Ebroin crossed the Seine at Pont-Sainte-Maxence, where his men killed Theuderic's soldiers who were on guard there. When the king learned of Ebroin's advance across the Seine he sent out other troops to ambush him, but these men met the same fate as those who had guarded the bridge at Sainte-Maxence. Next we learn of Leudesius' and Theuderic's flight from Ebroin, the seizure of the royal treasure at the villa of Baizieux, and finally of the king's capture at the royal villa of Crécy-en-Ponthieu.

Ebroin's success in this campaign resulted in his becoming mayor of the palace once again. Nevertheless, we continue to obtain detailed information in the *LHF* concerning doings at Theuderic's court after Ebroin became reestablished as mayor. For example, our author relates many details about Ebroin's and Theuderic's war against Peppin II and Duke Martin of Austrasia. We learn of the Neustrian's victory at Bois-Royal du Fays, Martin's escape to Laon, Ebroin's return with Theuderic to the royal villa at Ecry after the victory, Ebroin's negotiations with Martin, and of the former's oaths taken on empty boxes which were represented to Martin as containing relics. Finally, we are informed that Martin believed that Ebroin had truly sworn to give him safe conduct to visit the king at Ecry and that the mayor murdered the Duke and his followers at the royal court.

The account of affairs at Theuderic's court continues beyond Ebroin's fall, which is also described in detail and includes the name of his murderer. We learn that Ebroin was replaced as mayor of the palace by Waratto and his son Gislemar. The latter's character is well known to our author, who notes that he was "an able and diligent man" but one "who had a wild spirit and immature habits." Our author chronicles the vacillation of the Neustrians in finding a replacement for Waratto after both he and Gislemar were dead and hints at the role played by Waratto's wife, Anseflidis, in the ultimate selection of Berchar. Berchar, however, was a failure as a mayor, and he was defeated by Peppin at Tetry in 687. A short time after this battle, Berchar was murdered by some "time-servers" according to our author. Anseflidis is credited with encouraging Peppin to take over the duties of mayor of the palace of Neustria, and we learn that he established his man Nordebert to run affairs for King Theuderic. It is important to note that Fredegar's continuator, who was very well informed about the Austrasians, did not relate the name of the man Peppin assigned to handle things at Theuderic's court. It is clear that the details of court politics provided by our author go far beyond the tenure of any one mayor and are relatively comprehensive for the full reign of Theuderic III.

In addition to this detailed information on court politics, our author demonstrates an unparalleled knowledge of royal villas in Theuderic's kingdom and of events connected with them. For example, among those he mentions are Novient (modern Saint Cloud) where Chlodovald was buried, Compiègne where Chlotar I died, Chelles where Chilperic I was murdered, Baizieux where Ebroin captured Theuderic's royal treasure, Berny Rivière where Fredegund laid her plans to attack an Austrasian army, Crécy-en-Ponthieu, Ecry, Epinay-sur-Seine where Dagobert I died, Essonne, Vitry-en-Artois where Sigibert I was murdered, and Saint-Ouen-sur-Seine where Bishop Audoin of Rouen died in 684.

Perhaps understandable in a man who had this peculiar knowledge about royal villas in Theuderic's kingdom and was able to provide a detailed account of politics at the king's court, our author demonstrates a recognizable bias in favor of King Theuderic. The king is absolved of wrongdoing for which he might be held responsible as ruler. Rather than attribute blame to Theuderic as he does for example to Clovis II, our author articulates a variation on the theme of the "king's bad advisors". Thus we are told that Theuderic was deposed temporarily when "the Franks hostile to Ebroin prepared an ambush." It is, therefore, Ebroin's fault that Theuderic was deposed. In the same vein, the king is not held responsible for the brutal execution of Bishop Leudegar and his brother Gaerin or, for that matter, is Theuderic blamed for the, deceitful manner in which Duke Martin and his followers were lured to the royal court and murdered.

The thrust of this evidence suggests that the author of the *LHF* was a member of King Theuderic's entourage. Clerics, of course, were used in the writing offices of the Merovingian kings and our author demonstrates, as compared with his contemporaries, a particularly good command of Latin and a well-disciplined orthography. Concerning the latter, for example, he uses consistent spellings for names; this is virtually unique in Merovingian Gaul. Also unlike his contemporaries on the continent, the author of the *LHF* demonstrates a commitment to the grammar and form of classical Latin. For example, he uses *eius* and *eorum* in the correct classical manner and does not replace them with *suus*. Not only does this indicate his classical bent but it highlights his efforts not to permit the Romance (proto-French) which was his spoken language to corrupt his Latin.

A writer with the accomplishments exhibited by the author of the *LHF* may have served in Theuderic's court in a more important capacity than that of a simple writing office clerk. It is clear from the *LHF* that its author had some sort of special regard for Theuderic's youngest son, Childebert III

(694-711). In describing Childebert's accession to the king-ship, our author calls him a "famous man" and, in chronicling his death, he panegyrizes him: "The most glorious lord Childebert, a just king of good memory went to the Lord; he had reigned for seventeen years and was buried at the monastery of Choisy-au-Bac in the church of the protomartyr Saint Stephen." No other king who lived within the memory of our author is given such resounding praise. In fact, our author has nothing positive to say about the fame, accomplishments, or the burial places of any of the other monarchs who flourished from Dagobert I who died in 639 to the end of the *LHF* in 727. Curiously, however, our author tells us very little about the reign of Childebert in comparison with the detailed information he supplies about Theuderic's reign.

The evidence discussed above suggests the following hypotheses concerning the career of the man who wrote the *LHF*. He was probably educated at the monastery of Saint Vincent, concerning which he is so well informed but where he did not reside during that part of his life when he wrote the *LHF*. While a very young man and after a good education, he was probably recruited to serve in the entourage of Theuderic III. Our author's accomplishments as a Latinist and his academic discipline may have recom-mended him as a tutor for Childebert. After Theuderic's death in 690, our author seems to have left the royal court and thus he no longer had access to as much information on political intrigues as he had had before. This would therefore account for the decline in the detailed nature of the information presented in the *LHF* for the period after 690. During his later years our author went to live at the monastery of Saint Denis where he finished the *LHF* in 727. The decision to write a history of the Franks which emphasized the Neustrian side of things may well have stemmed from our author's connection with the royal court and perhaps was intended to encourage Neustrian patriotism at a time when the part of Gaul to which our author was most attached and loyal was faced with Austrasian domination.

§

The sources used by the author of the *LHF* can be considered in the two broad categories of written and oral; each of these may in turn be classified in subgroups. In terms of evaluating the author of the *LHF* as an historian, the most useful written sources are those identifiable accounts which still survive in their original form. From these we can ascertain in what instances our author altered his material and what he selected to use or omit, thereby introducing his own ideas or intentions in competition with the views of others. Among the sources in this group are Gregory of Tours' *History of the Franks*, Isidore of Seville's *Etymologies*, the addition to Marius of Avenches' *Chronicle*, and the shorter prologue to *Lex Salica*.

Of these works, Gregory's *History* is by far the most crucial to the composition of the *LHF*. Our author only drew material from the first six books of Gregory's ten-book *History*, but these six books provide the basic outline for the *LHF* until 584. It is true that our author uses only a very small percentage of the material which he found in Gregory's work, and it also should be noted that he adds information to some of the accounts he finds in the *History*. Much of the information he supplies independent of Gregory concerns geography. For example, he notes that Thuringia is in Germany, that the Charbonnière forest is located between Dispargum, Chlodio's stronghold, and the city of Tournai to the west of it, and that the battlefield of Vouillé where Clovis' armies defeated the Visigoths in 507 was near the river Clain. Our author also adds information to Gregory's account in the area of religious history. He tells us, for example, that Childebert built the church of Saint Vincent at Paris, that Clovis built the Church of Saint Peter at Paris, that Saint Cloud was buried at the villa of Novient, and that Saint Germanus was buried at the church of Saint Vincent.

These additions to Gregory's material are probably less significant than certain calculated factual omissions and variant interpretation of facts. We have already seen how our author's treatment of Fredegund is very different from that presented by Gregory. Another example is the treatment of King Guntram I in the *LHF*. Gregory provides a great deal of information about him and his kingdom but he is virtually ignored in the *LHF*. Chilperic I, Guntram's brother, is the villain of Gregory's *History*. Gregory calls him the "Nero and Herod of our time". Our author, however, leads the reader to be somewhat sympathetic toward him.

Those written sources used by the author of the *LHF* which are no longer extant are a second subgroup of materials we can identify. Thus, for example, we are told concerning Clovis II that "About his death nothing of historical worth may be said. Many writers condemn his end because they do not know the extent of his evil. Thus in uncertainty concerning it they refer from one to another." This strongly suggests that our author had access to several, or at least two, written accounts which dealt with at least a part of the reign of Clovis II. It will be remembered that Clovis desecrated the relics of Saint Denis and our author resided at the monastery of Saint Denis when he wrote the *LHF*. Thus it may be suggested that there was perhaps a chronicle written at the monastery during the reign of Clovis II to which our author had access when he wrote. There may also have been a *vita* of the saint available as well.

Also within the category of no longer extant written sources that our author used we may include epic literature. Accounts such as those elaborating Aurelian's efforts to arrange the marriage of Clotild and Clovis, Childeric's love affairs, and Fredegund's dalliance with Landeric were all probably part of a written epic tradition at the time at which the *LHF* was composed. Despite the obvious romantic tendency of these sources, there is undoubtedly a kernel of truth to be found in each episode.

Other epic materials available to our author, however, seem to have had no historical foundation at all. The most important example of these is the story of the Franks' Trojan origins. During the early middle ages, it was common for peoples to popularize stories concerning their past. Awareness of ethnicity in this period encouraged some groups to write history for the purpose of showing that they were as good as anyone else, if indeed not better. The prologue to the *Salic Law* contains the following glorification: "The famous Frankish people, whose founder is God, strong in war, faithful in its alliances, wise in counsel, well formed, completely loyal, handsome, audacious, quick, and fierce, and while still pagans sought by God's inspiration the key to knowledge.... Long live Christ who loves the Franks...for this people is brave and valiant, and threw off the Roman yoke."

This desire for glorification as seen in the story of the Franks' Trojan origins connects the Franks to the Romans by blood in that both have a common Trojan ancestor. By the mid-seventh century, tales of the Franks' Trojan origin were common in Gaul, and one was committed to writing by Fredegar. Our author, however, did not have access to Fredegar's version and that which appears in the *LHF* is considerably different from the one that appears in Fredegar. One unique element provided by the *LHF* in this epic concerns the Alans. In 407 the Alans decisively defeated the Franks. We have no reason, however, to believe that the Franks ever defeated the Alans. Our author ignores the Alan victory and tells a story about a Frankish victory over the

Alans which probably never occurred. The Alans, incidentally, are called "perverse" and "rotten".

The most important group of non-written sources used by our author are eyewitness accounts. At the court of Theuderic our author undoubtedly encountered men who could appraise him of events which took place in the days of Clovis II (d. 657) and even of things that had happened in the reigns of Dagobert I (d. 638) and Chlotar II (d. 629). The information concerning the attempt by the mayor of the palace Grimoald to place his own son on the Merovingian throne after deposing Dagobert II in 656 was probably obtained from oral rather than from written sources. The *LHF* is the earliest written account of the episode, and Fredegar either did not know about it or feared to write about it because of his connection with the Carolingians.

Chlotar II's epic victory in single combat against the Saxon Duke Bertoald has the ring of an embellished oral tradition which was likely to have been popular at the Neustrian court. This was also probably the case in regard to the story of the moving forest, Fredegund's camouflaged surprise attack against the Austrasians which served as the model through several intermediaries for Shakespeare's Birnam Wood.

Other oral traditions which probably are even more limited in the factual information they convey are also found in the *LHF*. Among these we may include episodes such as the one concerning the story of Clovis' horse and Saint Martin. We are told that Clovis gave his fastest horse to the church of Saint Martin before the battle of Vouillé in 507. After he won the battle, however, he wanted to get the horse back and thus offered the grooms one hundred gold pieces. The horse refused to move. Then Clovis doubled the price and the horse went to him. As the story goes, Clovis is made to remark, "Indeed, the blessed Martin is good in his help and careful in his business."

Not only does our author draw on the eyewitness accounts of his associates and other elements in the oral tradition, but he was probably an eyewitness himself to some of what he reports. Because he was very probably a functionary of some kind at the court of King Theuderic III from the early 670's, he could not avoid being exposed to some of the most important events of the time. Among these we may perhaps include the deposition of Theuderic and Ebroin and their being "dragged off by force," Theuderic's later flight from Ebroin, and perhaps even Ebroin's deceitful oath to Duke Martin taken on empty boxes that had been represented as containing relics. When seeking to evaluate the probable eyewitness evidence presented by our author, we must remember that he chronicled the vagaries of political fortune with a definite bias. He did his utmost to absolve King Theuderic of any charge of wrongdoing. One need only compare our author's assessment of Clovis II, as noted above, with his defense of Theuderic III to see the bias of the particular segment of the *LHF* to which our author was an eyewitness.

It should be emphasized that our author does not use either charters or epistolary evidence in obtaining information for the writing of the *LHF*. There is not the slightest hint in the *LHF* that he had access to or that he even considered using archival information. His treatment of chronology is cavalier to say the least. He often attributes far too many years or far too few years to a king's reign and is very rarely specific about exactly or even approximately how much time elapsed between the events he records. He frequently uses phrases such as "at that time", "some time having passed", and "at a following time". To be fair, however, it must be noted that our author's treatment of the sequence of events is generally accurate. This may perhaps suggest that he grasped and was concerned with certain essential elements of the notion of the linear development of events and even of historical causation.

The reader of the *LHF* will probably learn more about the early middle ages by trying to understand the author of this little history than by memorizing the facts that he presents. We may learn a great deal about our author's biases, values, and intentions if we can understand why he chose to include information on certain subjects while omitting other data. In short, through the *LHF* we have an entry into the mind of a man who lived in Gaul during the late seventh and early eighth centuries. Such opportunities for understanding early medieval people, even partially, are few and limited in scope. We should all try to make the most of them.

§

Bibliographical Note

The following works were used in preparing the Introduction: Bernard S. Bachrach, *A History of the Alans in the West* (Minneapolis, 1973); O.M. Dalton, *The History of the Franks by Gregory of Tours* (Oxford, 1927), 2 vols.; Louis Dupraz, *Contribution à l'histoire du Regnum Francorum* (Fribourg, 1948); Eugen Ewig, "Die fränkischen Teilreiche im 7 Jahrhundert (613-714)," *Trierer Zeitschrift,* XXII (1953), 85-144; B. Krusch, "Introduction" to the *LHF* which he edited: *Liber Historiae Francorum [Scriptores Rerum Merovingicarum: Monumenta Germanica Historica* (Hannover, 1888)]* vol. II (this edition serves also as the basis for the translation presented here); G. Kurth, *Histoire poétique des Mérovingiens* (Paris, 1893), *Clovis,* 2 vols. 2nd ed. (Paris, 1901), and *Etudes franques,* 2 vols. (Paris, 1919); A. Longnon, *Géographie de la Gaule au VIe siècle* (Paris, 1878); P. Taylor, *The Latinity of the Liber Historiae Francorum* (New York, 1924); and J.M. Wallace-Hadrill, *The Fourth Book of the Chronicle of Fredegar* (London, 1960).

Liber Historiae Francorum

1

[Concerning the Origin and Deeds of the Franks and their Frequent Struggles]

Let us set out the beginnings of the kings of the Franks and their origin and also the origins of the people and its deeds. There is in Asia the city of the Trojans in the region called Illium. This is where Aeneas reigned. The Trojans were a strong and brave people, the men were warriors and very difficult to discipline. They provoked conflict and stormy contention and fought successfully on their surrounding borders. But the kings of the Greeks rose up against Aeneas with a very large army and fought against Aeneas and there was a great deal of slaughter. Many Trojans fell in the battle and therefore Aeneas fled and shut himself up in the city of Illium. The Greeks besieged the city for ten years and when the city was conquered, the tyrant Aeneas fled to Italy to obtain men to carry on the fighting. Priam and Antenor, two of the other Trojan princes, embarked on ships with twelve thousand of the men remaining from the Trojan army. They departed and came to the banks of the Tanais [Don] river. They sailed into the Maeotian swamps [of the Sea of Azov], penetrated the frontiers of the Pannonias which were near the Maeotian swamps and began to build a city as their memorial. They called it Sicambria and lived there many years growing into a great people.

§

2

[Concerning the Alan people who rebelled against the
Emperor Valentinian, the Franks who conquered them, and
the remission of the tribute normally paid by the Franks]

At this time the perverse and rotten Alans revolted against
the Emperor Valentinian and the Roman people. Then
Valentinian moved a very large army from Rome, he went
against the Alans, entered battle with them and overcame
them and conquered. And the Alans having been defeated
fled beyond the Danube river and entered the Maeotian
swamps. In addition, the emperor said: "Whoever is able to
enter into these swamps and throw out this depraved people,
I will concede to them remission of the donatory tribute for
a period of ten years. Then the Trojans gathered together and
prepared ambushes in the way they had been taught and
knew. They entered the Maeotian swamps along with other
Romans, and they drove the Alans out and cut them down
with the edge of the sword. Because of the hardness and the
daring of their hearts the Emperor Valentinian called the
Trojans Franks. In the Attic tongue Frank means fierce.

§

3

[The Emperor sent tax collectors so that the Franks would pay tribute]

After ten years had passed, the previously mentioned Emperor Valentinian sent tax collectors along with a Duke Primarius of the Roman Senate to collect the customary tribute from the Frankish people. The Franks, however, since they were fierce and barbarous, having accepted useless counsel, they said to one another: "The emperor with the Roman army could not drive the Alans, a brave and rebellious people, from their hiding place in the swamp. Why then should we who conquered the Alans be the ones to pay tribute? Let us rise up together against this Primarius and the tax collectors, cut them down, and take all that they have with them. Then we will not give tribute to the Romans any more and we will be free always." Indeed, ambushes were set and the Franks killed the tax collectors.

§

4

[The Emperor moved the Roman army against the Franks,
concerning the Franks' arrival in the region of the
Rhine river, and their first king]

When the emperor learned about what happened he was
infuriated and burned with immeasurable anger. He ordered
into action an army of Romans and of other peoples with
Aristarcus as commander and sent it against the Frankish
army. There was a great deal of slaughter among both
peoples. The Franks realized, however, that they could not
hold out in this battle and they fled after many of them had
been cut to pieces and killed. Priam, the bravest of them, was
killed there. Thus they left Sicambria and traveled to the
farthest reaches of the Rhine river where the Germans'
strongholds are located. For many years they lived in this
region with their princes Marchomir, the son of Priam, and
Sunno, the son of Antenor. After Sunno died, however, they
took counsel so that they might have one king like other
peoples. Marchomir gave them this advice and they chose
Faramund, his son, and raised him up as the long-haired king
above them. Then they began to have laws which the leading
men of their people managed: Wisowast, Wisogast, Arogast,
and Salegast who were in charge of the localities on the other
side of the Rhine, namely Bothagm, Salechagm, and Wide-
chagm.

§

5

[Concerning the death of King Faramund and of his son
Chlodio and of the entry of the Huns into Gaul]

After King Faramund died they raised up into his father's
kingdom Chlodio his long-haired son. At this time they began
to have long-haired kings. Wisely, they came to the borders of
Thuringia and settled there. Therefore, King Chlodio lived in
the stronghold at Disbargo on the borders of the Thuringian
region of Germany. At that time Romans lived on the other
side of the Rhine up to the Loire river. The area beyond the
Loire was dominated by the Goths. The pagan Burgundians
who were in the grasp of the depraved Arian doctrine lived
near the Rhone river, which runs by the city of Lyons. King
Chlodio, however, sent spies from his Thuringian stronghold
at Disbargo to the city of Cambrai. Thus he crossed the
Rhine with a large army; he killed and chased away many
Romans. Then he entered the Charbonnière forest, took the
city of Tournai, and came up to the city of Cambrai where he
remained for a short time. The Romans whom he found there
he killed. After that he occupied the land up to the Somme
river. After Chlodio died, Merovech who was from his family
took over his kingdom. Chlodio had reigned for twenty years.
From this proper King Merovech, the kings of the Franks are
called Merovingians. It was at this time that the Huns crossed
the Rhine. They burned Metz, they destroyed Trier, penetrated the area around Tongres, and came up to Orléans. At

this time the holy Anianus, a man celebrated for his virtue, was bishop of Orléans. With the help of the Lord and through the prayers of the holy Anianus, Aetius, the Patrician of the Romans and Thorismud, the king of the Goths, came to Orléans. The Huns and their king Attila were driven from the city and soundly defeated.

§

6

[King Childeric was driven from his Kingdom]

Merovech had a son named Childeric who in turn was the father of the famous and very brave king Clovis. At this time, however, the Franks were pagans and fanatics, adoring idols and images and not the God of the heavens and the earth who created them. At that time King Aegidius who was a representative of the emperor of the Romans ruled in this part of Gaul. King Childeric, the son of Merovech, was given over to an excess of luxury, and he began to dishonor and seduce the daughters of the Franks over whom we ruled. They were indignant and very angry and wanted to throw him out of the kingdom and kill him. When he learned about this, Childeric called his friend Wiomad who was known to be prudent in counsel and asked him for his advice on how he thought the furor that was agitating the Franks could be calmed. Childeric and Wiomad arranged a signal between them. By this sure sign which only the two of them knew, Childeric would know if and indeed when he might return in peace. Thus they divided a gold coin in half. King Childeric carried one half with him and Wiomad held onto the other half saying: "When I send this other part to you, you will know that through me the Franks have made peace with you, and that you may return safely." Then King Childeric went to Thuringia and hid there safely with King Bisinus and his wife.

§

7

[The Franks established above them the Roman Aegidius and they threw out Childeric and later recalled him]

After Childeric left, the Franks, following bad counsel, established above them to rule the kingdom Aegidius the prince of the Romans. When Aegidius had reigned for eight years, Wiomad became his follower and joined himself to him in friendship so that while with him he might learn what he planned. Craftily, Aegidius was encouraged to oppress the other Franks. Upon hearing this counsel, Aegidius began to oppress them sharply. The Franks, however, were turned to fear and resistance. Again they sought counsel from Wiomad as to what they should do. He said to them: "Do you not remember how the oppressing Romans threw out your people and drove them from their lands? You, indeed, threw out your proper and wise king and raised above you that overbearing and proud soldier of the emperor; you did not take good counsel but very bad counsel." They answered: "That was very rash of us. Aegidius causes us to repent of having done this against our king. If only we could find Childeric so that he might reign over us in peace." Then the friend, Wiomad, sent his part of the gold piece which earlier he had divided with Childeric to the king. Childeric, knowing the meaning of the sign of the half of the gold piece, understood the sure indication that the Franks wanted him back very much. Therefore, after he was asked, he returned to his kingdom. While he was in Thuringia, however, King Childeric committed adultery with Queen Basina, the wife of King Bisinus. When Childeric was received back in the kingdom of the Franks the Roman prince Aegidius was expelled from above the kingdom. Basina the queen of King Bisinus of the Thuringians, moreover, left her husband, and came to Childeric. When the questioner asked what she wanted and why she had come to him from so distant a region, she is said to have answered: "I know your quality and your handsomeness and that you are able and wise. Therefore I came so that I could live with you. If, indeed, I knew someone better than you even if he were beyond the sea, I would seek him out and I would marry him. Rejoicing, he joined her to him in marriage. She conceived by him and she had a son and called him Clovis. He was the greatest of all the kings of the Franks and a very brave warrior.

§

8

[The city of Cologne is captured, the death of Aegidius,
and concerning Adovagrius, Duke of the Saxons]

In these days the Franks took the city of Agripina on the
Rhine and they called it Cologne as if coloni inhabited it.
They killed many Romans who were Aegidius' partisans
there. Aegidius himself fled and escaped. Then the Franks
came to the city of Trier on the Moselle river. They
devastated the land and they began to burn the city. After
these things happened, Aegidius, king of the Romans, died.
Syagrius, his son, ruled in his kingdom; he established the
capital of his kingdom in the city of Soissons. Then King
Childeric mustered the Frankish host in a very large army. He
came up to the city of Orléans and also devastated the lands
around it. Adovagrius, the duke of the Saxons, with a naval
force came by water up to the city of Angers and he burned
the land and slaughtered many of the people in the city.
Then Adovagrius left Angers and King Childeric of the
Franks got together his army and came there. He killed
Count Paul who was there at the time. Childeric took the city
and Paul's house which was in the city he burned with fire.
Then Childeric returned home.

§

9

[The death of Childeric and Clovis' war with Syagrius]

After this, King Childeric died. He had reigned for twenty-four years. Clovis, his son, manfully received the kingdom of the Franks. After Clovis had ruled for five years, Syagrius, son of Aegidius, still resided in the city of Soissons which his father had held. Clovis and his relative Ragnachar with an army went against Syagrius. They came together in battle fighting bravely against each other. Syagrius, however, realized that his army had been badly cut up and thus took flight and fled to Alaric, king of the Goths, at the city of Toulouse. Then Clovis sent his messengers to Alaric so that the latter should return Syagrius; if he did not wish to return him, however, he was told that he had better prepare for war. Alaric feared the anger of the Franks and therefore handed Syagrius over to Clovis' messengers. When Syagrius was presented to Clovis, he ordered him to be killed. Clovis then took over Syagrius' entire kingdom and treasure.

§

10

[Concerning the bishop's request to Clovis for the return
of the ewer and how the conquered Thuringians paid tribute]

At this time many churches were looted by Clovis' army.
He was a fanatic and a pagan at that time. So it happened
that his troops took from a church a ewer of great size and
immense beauty along with many other things that are used
in the church service as well as many ornaments. The bishop
of the church, however, sent his messengers to the king,
asking that if the other vases from the church might not be
returned would Clovis perhaps order the return of the ewer.
The king, after hearing this request, said to the church
messengers: "Follow us up to the city of Soissons where we
will divide all the booty that has been taken." When the ewer
comes to me as a part of my share, I will do what the bishop
asks." When the king came to the city of Soissons, he asked
that all of the booty that they had acquired be brought into
the midst of the group. Then he said, "I ask that you my very
brave and noble warriors do not refuse to give me this ewer."
After the king said these things, the Franks who were of good
spirit said: "Glorious king, all that you see is yours, and we
are to be commanded by your lordship. What seems good to
you, do that, for no one dare resist your power." They said
this courteously; one foolish Frank, however, with a shout
raised his axe, that is his francisca, and struck the ewer

saying: "You may take nothing, king, except that which the lot brings to you." Everyone was astounded, the king bore his injury patiently, and gave the ewer which he accepted to the church messenger. King Clovis, however, kept his anger in his heart. A year having passed, King Clovis ordered his entire army to come in full arms to the field of Mars to show the brightness of their weapons. There, indeed, the king went around inspecting the entire force. He came to the man, who before had struck the ewer and said to him: "No one has more neglected and filthy arms than you. That is because neither your shield, nor your spear, nor your axe is of use to you." The king took the man's francisca, which is an axe, and threw it on the ground. When the man bent down to pick it up, the king suddenly raised his hands and drove his own axe into the man's head and said: "This is what you did to the ewer last year at Soissons." After the man died, the king ordered the rest of the army to leave the camp in peace and return to their own lands. Because of what Clovis had done there rose in the Frankish people great fear and dread. After ten years of his reign had passed, Clovis gathered together a large force of Franks to attack Thuringia. He went into Thuringia and defeated the Thuringians imposing great losses on them. The Thuringian people were beaten, their entire land was devastated, and they were made to pay tribute.

§

11

[Aurelianus, Clovis' legate, dressed like a poor stranger
and arranged for Clovis' betrothal to Clotild]

At this time Gundioc, king of the Burgundians, who was
of the family of King Athanaric, was in power. His four sons
were Gundobad, Godigisel, Chilperic, and Gundomar. Gundobad killed his brother Chilperic with a sword and he had the
latter's wife drowned in the water by tying a stone around
her neck. Chrona, the elder of Chilperic's two daughters, had
become a nun and Gundobad exiled her. The younger
daughter who was named Clotild, Gundobad kept at home.
Since Clovis frequently sent legations into Burgundy, it
happened that the girl, Clotild, was noticed by the legates.
These legates noticed Clotild's beauty, grace, and intelligence,
and told Clovis. After Clovis learned all of this, he sent his
legate Aurelianus on another mission to Gundobad to ask for
his niece. Clotild was a Christian. On a certain Sunday when
Clotild came to the solemn mass, Aurelianus, Clovis' messenger, left his good clothes with his followers in the woods and
put on poor clothes. Then he sat down before the table for
doling out alms in the church in the midst of the poor. After
the solemn mass ended, Clotild, according to custom, went
alone to give alms to the poor. When she came to
Aurelianus, who was disguised as a poor man, she put one
gold piece in his hand. He kissed the girl's hand and drew

back her cloak. After this she went to her chamber and sent
her servant to call the pilgrim. Aurelianus held the ring that
Clovis had given him in his hand and kept the rest of the
betrothal ornaments in the sack in which he had brought
them. This sack he left behind the door of the room. Clotild
said to him: "Tell me young man why do you disguise
yourself as a poor man and for what reason did you pull back
my cloak?" He replied: "Your servant begs to speak with you
in secret." She said: "Speak." Then he said: "My lord Clovis,
king of the Franks, sent me to you. He wishes to have you
for his queen. See this ring and other betrothal ornaments
which I have brought!" Then he looked back behind the door
of the room. He did not find his sack and this trouble began
to sadden him. She solicitously inquired and said: "Who took
the poor man's sack?" It was found and she received the
hidden betrothal ornaments. After she accepted the ring
which King Clovis had sent by Aurelianus, she placed it in her
uncle's treasury. After this she sent greetings to Clovis,
saying: "It is not permitted for a Christian woman to marry a
pagan, therefore do not let our betrothal be known. Whatever
my Lord God orders, I confess that I will do. Go in peace."
Upon his return, Aurelianus reported this to his lord.

§

12

[King Clovis sends to Gundobad for his betrothed Clotild]

In the following year, Clovis sent his legate Aurelianus to Gundobad for his betrothed Clotild. Hearing this, Gundobad, terrified in his heart, said: "Since Clovis at no time knew my niece, you, all my brave counselors and loyal Burgundian friends may know how the king of the Franks seeks a provocation." Then he said to Aurelianus: "You have come to spy upon our house seeking a provocation. Report to your lord, Clovis, that he has lied in a vain effort to obtain my niece as his betrothed." Speaking steadily, Aurelianus said to him: "My lord king, Clovis, orders therefore that if you do not wish to give his betrothed to him, that you should prepare a place for him and designate where you wish and in that place Clovis will receive his betrothed. If, however, you do not comply, Clovis is preparing to come with an army of Franks to your meeting." Gundobad replied: "Let him come wherever he wishes. I am prepared to go against him with a large army of Burgundians so that his ruin may come in front of many people in public and so that the blood which stains his hands from the killing of so many will be avenged." When the Burgundians heard this exchange they feared greatly the anger of the Franks and of Clovis. They advised Gundobad by saying: "May the king perhaps ask his officers and his chamberlain if there were not some gifts brought at some time in an ingenious manner by a legate of King Clovis. Thus Clovis, to whom wasteful extravagance is very angering, will

not have a pretext to go against your people and your
kingdom and so that you may be able to overcome him." As
customary, the Burgundians gave their advice to the king.
They searched, and indeed, they found a ring inscribed with
the name and image of Clovis in King Gundobad's treasury.
Then a very much saddened King Gundobad ordered that
Clotild be brought to him so that he might inquire about this
matter. She said: "I know, my lord king, that in previous
years small gifts of gold were brought to you by Clovis'
messengers. It so happened that a little ring was placed in my
hand, your little servant. I then hid it in your treasury." He
said: "This was done innocently and without advice." Then
he grasped her angrily and handed her over to Aurelianus.
The latter with his followers received Clotild very joyfully
and took her to King Clovis at the city of Soissons in Francia.
King Clovis also rejoiced and joined her to him in marriage.
When it was late that day, at the time when by custom the
marriage was to be consummated, Clotild, moved by her
accustomed prudence, confessed to God and said: "Now is
the time my lord king that you hear your servant so that you
may deem to concede what I pray for before I become a part
of your family and pass under your lordship." The king
answered: "Ask what you wish and I will grant it." And she
asked, saying: "First, I ask that you believe in the God of
heaven, the omnipotent Father, who created you. Second,
confess Lord Jesus Christ, His son, the King of all kings sent
by the Father of heaven, who redeemed you. Third, believe
in the Holy Spirit, confirmer and illuminator of all the just.
Acknowledge His complete ineffable majesty and co-eternal
omnipotence. Having acknowledged, believe. Give up your
meaningless idols which are not gods but worthless carvings.
Burn them and restore the holy churches that you have
burned. And remember also that I ask that you should
demand the estate of my father and of my mother whom my
uncle Gundobad evilly killed. Thus the Lord may avenge

their blood." Then Clovis answered: "Only one thing that you have asked remains difficult and that is your request that I give up my gods and follow your God. Anything else that you ask, I will do as the opportunity arises." And she said: "I ask this above all else, that you worship the omnipotent Lord God who is in heaven."

§

13

[Clovis again sends to Gundobad for Clotild's Treasure]

Again Clovis sent Aurelianus into Burgundy to Gundobad because of the treasure of his queen Clotild. Gundobad became very angry and asked: "Is there anything in my kingdom or in my treasury that should be given into Clovis' hand? Did you not understand, Aurelianus, that you were not to come into my kingdom to ascertain my wealth? For the welfare of your prince, I swear, return to him quickly and leave me, if you do not I will kill you." Aurelianus answered him, saying: "My lord, King Clovis, lives as do the Franks who are with him, therefore I do not fear your threats while my lord flourishes. Thus your own son, King Clovis, asks where he may come for the treasure of his wife, my lady." Therefore, the Burgundians, according to custom, gave counsel to Gundobad, their king. They said: "Give to your niece any of the riches in your treasury that are hers because this is deemed to be just. Thus you will have an alliance and friendship with King Clovis and the Frankish people. If you do not do this they will attack our land vigorously, because they are strong and a fierce people without God." Gundobad, hearing their counsel, handed over to Aurelianus for Clovis the greater part of his treasure: gold, silver, and many ornaments. And he said: "Is there anything else that remains, except perhaps that I divide my entire kingdom with Clovis?" And he said to Aurelianus: "Return to your lord since you have that which you may bring to him, the many gifts that you have not worked for." Aurelianus then said: "Your son is my lord King Clovis; everything is yours in common." The wise Burgundians said: "Long live the king who has such followers." Aurelianus returned to his lord in Francia with a great deal of treasure. By a concubine, King Clovis had a son by the name of Theuderic.

§

14

[Concerning Clotild's requests that Clovis might believe
in the King of kings]

At this time Clovis enlarged his kingdom, extending it up to the Seine. At a later time he occupied the land up to the Loire river. Aurelianus received the stronghold of Melun and the entire region as a dukedom. Then Clotild conceived by Clovis and had a son whom she wished to consecrate with baptism. Since the lord king did not believe in God, the queen begged him daily, but he did not wish to hear her. Meanwhile, the queen prepared to baptize the boy. She adorned the church with hangings and curtains, so that they might bring the king to believe. Moreover, the boy was baptized. While he was still in white, however, this boy, whom she called Ingomir, fell sick and died. As a result of this the king was very much saddened. With vehement recrimination, he said: "If the boy had been dedicated in the name of my gods, surely he would have survived. Because he was baptized in the name of your God, he could not live." The queen answered: "I give thanks to God, because He did not regard me as unworthy, that He deigned to receive into His kingdom the first-born child from my uterus. For this reason, moreover, I have no pain in my heart. After this it so happened that she bore another son whom in baptism she called Chlodomer. When he too began to die, the king said:

"Nothing else is possible except that he will have the same
fate as his brother, that having been baptized in the name of
your Christ he will quickly die." But as a result of the
queen's prayers and the Lord's unsurpassed mercy the boy
recovered his health. The queen, indeed, did not stop asking
the king to follow the true God and to give up the worthless
idols that he cared for. But in no way could she move his soul
to believe. Then it happened during a war against the
Alamans and Sueves, that Clovis was compelled to
acknowledge that which he had denied before.

§

15

[The war against the Alamans in which Clovis was compelled by necessity to call upon God to help him and his baptism by Saint Remigius]

It is indeed a fact that in the fighting between the army of the Franks and that of the Alamans, a very great many of Clovis' people were killed. Aurelianus, seeing this, said to the king: "My lord king, believe only in the Lord of heaven whom your queen proclaims." Indeed, Clovis raised his eyes to heaven and moved to tears, said: "Oh Jesus Christ whom Clotild, my wife, proclaims to be the son of God, You who are said to aid those in trouble, I a faithful man ask Your help so that if You give me victory over this enemy and Your strength has been put to the test which people claim that You have, I will be baptized. I wish to believe in You, the true God, and I call upon Your Lordship, so that I might be free of my enemies." He proclaimed this while he was praying, and the Alamans turned their backs and slipped away in flight. When they saw that their king was dead, they submitted to Clovis, saying: "Have mercy lord king we pray, let no more people perish, we are already yours." Then the king ordered the already imminent slaughter to cease. He initiated and carried out putting both the Alamans and their lands under the yoke of tribute. After the victory had been won, he returned to Francia and to his queen and told her

how through calling upon the name of Jesus Christ he
merited gaining victory. This happened in the fifteenth year
of Clovis' reign. Then the queen secretly called to her the
holy Remigius, bishop of the city of Rheims, and asked him
to show the road to salvation to the king. Remigius asked
Clovis to come to be baptized. But Clovis said: "Blessed
father, I hear you freely. But one thing remains. The people
who follow me do not want to give up their gods.
Nevertheless, I will go out to encourage them according to
your word." When the king came together with the people,
he began to exhort them. He spoke out about the
unsurpassed mercy of God and of His power. With one voice
the Frankish people said: "We will give up mortal gods,
glorious king, and we are prepared to believe in the true
immortal God whom Remigius proclaims." Remigius was also
filled with great joy and ordered a baptismal font to be
prepared. Cloths upon which holy scenes had been painted
were hung in the streets, the baptistry was put in order, and
balsam-scented candles wafted redolent odors. Thus the Lord
helped by giving the people grace so that they might learn
how to dispose themselves to the scents of paradise. The new
Constantine came to baptism, having denied the ways of the
devil. As he entered upon baptism, God's holy man spoke
thus with fine rhetoric: "Bow your penitent neck, Sicamber;
adore that which you have burned, burn that which you have
adored." The holy Remigius, moreover, was a very wise man,
a rhetorician, and outstanding in his great virtue. Thus the
king confessed his belief in the omnipotent God in Trinity.
He was baptized in the name of the Father, and the Son, and
the Holy Spirit. He was anointed with holy oil and with the
sign of the cross of our Lord Jesus Christ. From among his
fighting men more than three thousand were baptized. His
sisters, who were named Albofledis and Landechildis, were
baptized that day. Afterward all of the Frankish people were
baptized.

§

16

[Where the Burgundians were defeated by Clovis and how
they subjected themselves to his lordship. Concerning men
who it is said were eaten by beasts]

After this Clovis went against Gundobad and Godegisel
his brother with a large army of Franks. When the brothers
heard this they mobilized many of the Burgundian people
and prepared for battle. Having come to Dijon, a fortified
place, on the River Ouche, Clovis, Gundobad and Godegisel
fought there vigorously. After many Burgundians had been
killed, they turned their backs in flight. As Clovis was
accustomed to doing, he emerged as the victor. The army of
the Burgundians having been shattered, Gundobad and
Godegisel turned in flight and barely escaped. Gundobad
entered Avignon, a city on the Rhone, and there he shut
himself up. Clovis, having followed him there, laid siege so
that he might force him from the city and destroy him. When
Gundobad heard this, he was terrified with fear. He feared
that sudden death might come to him. Gundobad had with
him there a Roman of the senatorial class named Aridius.
This Aridius was quick-witted and also wise. Gundobad called
Aridius to him and said: "Because these barbarians have
come against us with the aim of killing us and laying waste to
the whole land, troubles surround me on all sides and I do
not know what I should do." To this Aridius answered: "You

had best calm the savagery of this man, lest you perish. Therefore, if it is pleasing in your eyes, I will feign to desert you and go over to Clovis. I will go to him and bring things about so that neither you nor your land is ruined. You have only to worry about satisfying all the demands which by my advice he will make on you. Do this until the Lord of His goodness deigns to make your cause triumph." Gundobad replied: "I will do whatever you ask." After this was said, Aridius said farewell and departed. Upon coming to King Clovis, he said: "Behold me, my pious king, I am your humble slave, who has left the miserable Gundobad to come under your power. If now your piety deigns to receive me, you and your heirs will find in me an honest and faithful follower." Clovis thus made Aridius one of his retainers, and kept him near his person. Aridius told good stories, gave good counsel, was just in his judgement, and faithful in his service. While Clovis was still besieging the city with his army, Aridius said: "O king, if in the majesty of your high position you deign to hear from me a few words of humble advice, though, indeed, you have little need of counsel, I will offer them in all loyalty. This advice will be valuable both to you and to the regions which you may wish to cross. Why," Aridius said, "do you keep your army in the field besieging this city when your foe is positioned in a very strong place? You lay waste to the fields, despoil the meadows, cut the vines, and chop down the olive trees, and yet you have not really weakened Gundobad's position. Rather, send envoys to him and impose a yearly tribute, so that this region can be saved from ruin, and you will always be lord over those paying tribute. If he should refuse, then do what you please." The king accepted this advice and ordered his army to return home. Then he sent an embassy to Gundobad. He ordered him to pay yearly the tribute which was now imposed upon him. Gundobad paid it immediately and promised to pay in the future as well. Thus Clovis returned home carrying the treasure, **truly** the victor. At this time the city of Vienne was frequently shaken by earthquakes. Many of the churches and many of the houses were shaken and knocked down. At Vienne many beasts — wolves, bears, and deer — entered the gates and wandered about without fear through the whole city eating up many people during the year. At the approach of the solemn holy Sunday of Easter, the holy Mamertus who was bishop of the city was celebrating mass at night when the royal palace that was in the city was burned by divine fire. When after these events, the day of the Lord's Ascension drew near, the holy man of God proclaimed a three day fast, the people came forth with a sigh and contrite soul to celebrate the innumerable ages in eternal time. Then all these troubles and problems ceased. Finally, all the churches of God and priests imitated this example, and up to the present the three day litany is practiced everywhere.

§

17

**[Concerning God's miracles revealed to Clovis as a result
of which he defeated the Goths and killed Alaric]**

Then King Clovis came to the city of Paris, and said to his
queen and to his people: "It bothers me a great deal that the
Arian Goths hold the best part of Gaul. Let us move against
them with God's help and drive them from the land and
because it is very much better put it under our sway. This
counsel pleased the Frankish magnates. Then Queen Clotild
gave counsel to the king, saying: "Let the Lord God give
victory into the hand of my lord king. Listen to your servant,
and we will build a church in honor of the most blessed Saint
Peter, prince of the apostles, so that he may be a helper to
you in the war." And the king said: "This speech pleases me,
we will do it." Then the king threw his axe, that is his
francisca, straight in front of him, and said: "So the church
of the blessed apostles will be built here, when with the
Lord's help we return." Then the king assembled his whole
army of the Frankish people and marched on Poitiers where
Alaric, king of the Goths, happened to be. A large part of
Clovis' troops had to cross the territory of Tours. Thus the
king ordered, because of his reverence for Saint Martin, that
nothing except grass might his men dare to take for the
sustenance of their horses. And in addition, the king ordered
messengers to go to the church of Saint Martin with many

gifts and with his very fastest horse, which he loved very much, and Clovis said: "Go and perhaps some word of victory from the holy scriptures will be made known." Then Clovis gave the messengers gifts and said: "If You, O Lord, help me, and if You will give into my hands this unbelieving people, may You deign to give me a sign at the entrance to the basilica of the blessed Martin, so that I may know that You will show your servant your favor." Clovis' followers came to the church of the blessed Saint Martin and as they passed over the threshold, the primicirius of the church turned to this antiphone, saying: "You have girded me, O Lord, with strength in battle; You have subjected under me those who rose up against me. You have made my enemies turn their backs to me and You have destroyed those who hate me." Thus they heard that psalm; the messengers gave thanks to the Lord, and after handing over the king's horse and other gifts, they joyfully and with exultation returned and gave their news to the king. When Clovis reached the Vienne river with his army, he found no place to cross it because it had been swollen by heavy rains. That night Clovis prayed to the Lord so that He might show him the way. At dawn a very large doe entered the river in front of them at God's bidding. She showed the way and the army followed. When the king came to the neighborhood of Poitiers and after his camp had been set up at some distance from the church of Saint Hilary, a fiery light was seen to come from the church that night. It appeared over the tents and signified that King Clovis was supported by the strength of Saint Hilary. Moreover, the king ordered that his army might take neither food nor any payment nor carry off any other booty. Then King Clovis encountered Alaric, king of the Goths, on the field of Vouillé on the banks of the river Clain at the tenth milestone outside of Poitiers. The two sides fought against each other and the Goths with their king very severely wounded turned their backs. Clovis, as he was accustomed, emerged the victor.

And when he had killed Alaric, two Goths came against him with lances from each side, but because of his coat of mail, which protected him, they did not kill him. Moreover, the Lord helped him in everything which he did. There died on the field of battle a great number of the people of the Auvergne who had come there with Duke Apollinaris. Many senators were cut down by the swords of the Franks in the battle. From this battle Amalaric, son of Alaric, escaped by flight. He wisely ruled the remaining part of his father's kingdom in Spain. Clovis, moreover, sent his own son Theuderic through Albi, the Rodez region, and on into the Auvergne. Crossing these territories, Theuderic subjugated to his father's domination the whole country from the Gothic to the Burgundian borders. Alaric had reigned for twelve years. Clovis spent the entire winter in Bordeaux and carried off a great many of Alaric's treasures from Toulouse. After all the cities had been taken, coming to the city of Angoulême, the Lord showed Clovis so much favor that the walls fell down by themselves before the king. After he killed the Goths who were there, Clovis seized the city and subjugated the entire region around it. He ordered Franks to remain at Saintes and Bordeaux to destroy the Goths. Then Clovis returned to the city of Tours. He gave many gifts to the church of Saint Martin. He wanted the horse which before he had given to the church to be returned to him so he gave the grooms a hundred gold pieces for it. Since the horse had been a gift, it never moved. And Clovis said: "Give another hundred gold pieces." At once the horse went free. Then joyfully the king said: "Indeed, the blessed Martin is good in his help and careful in business." Clovis received letters from the Emperor Anastasius conferring on him the consulship, and in the church of the blessed Martin he dressed in the purple tunic and set the gold diadem upon his head. Then mounting his horse, he handed out and kindly gave gold and silver to the people in the atrium, that is between the city and the church of the blessed Martin. From that day on Clovis was called consul and Augustus. He left Tours and came to Paris, where he established the seat of his government.

§

18

[Clovis' war against his relative Ragnachar]

Finally, Clovis moved against Ragnachar, his relative. This Ragnachar was then at the city of Cambrai living in luxury. He had as a counselor a certain man named Farron who was corrupted in the same manner. It was said about Ragnachar that when anyone brought a gift or food, he said: "These are for me and my counselor Farron." Because of this the Franks were indignant. The men in Ragnachar's following agreed to go against him with Clovis. Thus Clovis gave belts and armlets of gold to Ragnachar's leudes as gifts so that they would call him in against their lord. The gold, however, was really only cleverly gilded copper. Clovis moved his army against Ragnachar, his relative. Ragnachar sent out scouts to learn which army was bigger, his or that led by Clovis. These men lied and answered: "Your amy is strong enough for you and your counselor Farron." Clovis and Ragnachar came together in battle and fought vigorously. Ragnachar saw his army defeated and prepared to flee. But he was caught by the traitors. His hands were tied behind his back and the same was done to his brother Ricchar. Both were then handed over to Clovis. Clovis then said to Ragnachar: "Why have you disgraced our people by allowing yourself to be bound? It would have been better for you to have died." Then Clovis raised his axe and buried it in Ragnachar's head, and he died.

After this, Clovis turned to Ricchar and said: "If you had aided your brother, he would not have been bound." Similarly, Clovis struck him in the head, and he died. After this had been done, their betrayers learned that the gold which Clovis had given them was false. They told this to the king. He answered: "You who hand over your lord to die deserve to receive such gold. Let it be enough that I give you your lives and that you are not tortured to death." When they heard this, they chose to receive Clovis' grace saying that it is enough that they be left alive. This above-mentioned Ragnachar had relatives. Rignomer, the brother of Ragnachar and Ricchar, was killed at Le Mans by the order of King Clovis. When these were dead Clovis took all of their kingdom and their treasures. He killed many kings and a great number of his relatives.

§

19

[Concerning the death of Clovis and how his four sons
succeeded to his kingdom. Concerning the Danes
who invaded Gaul]

After all of these events, Clovis died at Paris in peace and
was buried in the church of the holy apostle Peter which he
and his queen had built. Clovis died in the fifth year after the
battle in which he fought against King Alaric of the Goths.
He reigned for thirty years. From the passing of Saint Martin
to the passing of King Clovis, there were one hundred twelve
years. After the death of her husband, Queen Clotild
frequently came to Tours and remained a very long time at
the church of the blessed Martin where she served the Lord.
She rarely visited Paris. After the death of King Clovis his
four sons Theuderic, Chlodomer, Childebert, and Chlothar
divided his kingdom among themselves equally. Theuderic
already had a son named Theudebert, a boy of talent and
ability. These kings were raised up into positions of great
power. Amalaric, son of Alaric, king of the Goths asked to
marry their sister. This request they did not deny, but they
sent her to him with many rich ornaments, and Amalaric
took her in marriage to himself. At this time the Danes and
their king, Chochilaich, crossed the seas with their ships and
came to Gaul. They landed in the Chatuarian region which
belonged to Theuderic and devastated everything. The

prisoners they took filled their ships. After they returned to their ships on the open sea, their king remained on shore. When the news was brought to Theuderic, he sent his son Theudebert into those parts with a large army. Theudebert reached the Danes, fought against them, defeated them with a great deal of slaughter, and killed their king. Theudebert then took the spoils from the Danes and restored them to the people in his territory.

§

20

[How Chlodomer, Childebert and Chlotar went to war against the Burgundians]

In these days Queen Clotild came to Paris and said to her sons: "My sons, do not make me regret that I brought you up sweetly. I pray that you avenge my indignant injury and the death of my father and of my mother." When they heard this they became very angry and advanced with a large army into Burgundy against King Sigismund and King Godomar, the sons of King Gundobad. At that time King Sigismund built in Burgundy the monastery of the holy martyrs of Agaune, Saint Maurice and his 6,600 companions. Moreover, Sigismund and Godomar moved the Burgundian army against King Chlodomer and the brothers Childebert and Chlotar, the sons of Clovis. The armies fought against each other and the Burgundians having been defeated, fled with Godomar. Sigismund, indeed, fled to the monastery at Agaune. Then he was taken prisoner with his wife and sons by Chlodomer and was kept imprisoned in the territory of Orléans. Chlodomer put them in jail and ordered them to be kept confined. The blessed bishop Avitus, however, who was then a holy man of God, an abbot in the city of Orléans, begged Chlodomer not to kill Sigismund and his family; but Chlodomer did not wish to listen to him. Then Chlodomer killed Sigismund and his wife and his children and threw them into a well in a place which is called Saint-Péravy la Colombe.

§

21

[Chlodomer again defeated the Burgundians and was killed]

After this Chlodomer again gathered his army and moved into Burgundy against Godomar. And when they came with a large army into the region of Vienne in a place which is called Vézeronce, Godomar deployed his men and fought against Chlodomer. The Burgundians were decisively beaten, and with Godomar they fled. When Chlodomer pursued them too forcefully and got too far from his men because of the speed of his horse he ended up in the midst of the Burgundians. They attacked him from all sides, he fell and died. The Franks seeing this were filled with a great deal of pain and anger. They pursued Godomar and killed him, the Burgundians perished, and the whole region was devastated. Then the Franks returned home. When Chlotar heard this he took his brother's wife, Guntheuc, as his own wife. Queen Clotild took over the raising of Chlodomer's orphan sons Theudovald and Chlodovald, and kept them with her.

§

22

[Concerning the great slaughter of the Thuringian people
and of their King Hermenfred by the Franks]

At this time Theuderic and Theudebert, his son, and King
Chlotar with the army of the Franks crossed the Rhine and
marched into Thuringia against Hermenfred, king of the
Thuringians. The Thuringians, hearing of this, dug ditches as
a trick and covered these over with sod. When the Franks
entered battle, learning that their horses were tripped up they
were very angry. Hermanfred, however, fled with the
Thuringians up to the Unstrut river, the Franks pursued him
there. There the Thuringians having reformed their forces
went against the Franks. So many of the Thuringians were
killed that the river was filled up by their bodies and the
Franks crossed over them as if over a bridge and trampled
them under foot. The Franks depopulated the entire region,
devastating it and taking captives. Hermanfred barely escaped
by flight. The Franks, moreover, returned home with a great
deal of booty and spoil. Hermanfred had two brothers named
Balderic and Bertechar. After this, Theuderic again gave his
oath to King Hermanfred and had him come to him at the
city of Tolbiac. When they were talking together high up on
the wall of the city, Hermanfred fell to the ground and was
killed. Theuderic then sought to have Hermanfred's young
children killed.

§

23

[Concerning the war Childebert waged against the Goths
and the killing of Amalaric]

When Childebert was in the Auvergne, his sister, the wife
of King Amalaric of the Goths (the name of the girl was
Queen Chrodchild), sent envoys from Spain to him saying
that a great many evil things were being carried on against the
true Catholic faith. For when she went to pray at the Church
of Christ, Amalaric threw dung and many kinds of refuse at
her and he beat her so much that she sent to her brother a
handkerchief smeared with blood, saying: "Avenge my
hardships and injuries, sweet brothers, dear lords." When
Childebert heard this, he was roused to very great anger. He
gathered a very large force, marched into Spain, and started a
war with Amalaric. The Goths having been seriously
defeated, Amalaric turned in flight to the ships he had
prepared for the retreat. When he tried to reach the ships,
however, he was followed by Childebert's army. Seeing that
he was thwarted, Amalaric tried to flee to the Church of the
Christians; but before he went through the entrance of the
church a certain Frank struck him with a spear, and he died
there. Then Childebert devastated Spain, entered the city of
Toledo, and carried off from there great treasures. He then
returned home with his sister. I do not know the immediate
danger from which weakly she died while on the journey. She

was taken to Paris and buried next to her father in the church of Saint Peter. Childebert, indeed, carried off among other treasures, church plate: the vase of Solomon, sixty very precious chalices, fifteen patens, twenty covers for the Gospels, all made from pure gold and beautifully decorated with precious stones. Indeed, he did not wish these things to be broken up so he gave all of them to churches, distributing them among all the churches.

§

24

[Because of evil advice, Childebert and Chlotar dragged off their nephews and killed them. Then they invaded the kingdom of the boys' father]

In these days Queen Clotild resided at Paris, and King Childebert saw that the sons of his older brother Chlodomer were being taken care of by the queen, his own mother, and that she was overly attentive to them. Childebert, thinking that she intended to make them kings, said to Chlotar, his brother: "Our mother has the sons of our brother with her and wants to hold on to them and wishes to raise them up in the kingdom of our brother. Having taken counsel, we must seize the boys to decide what to do with them. Whether we must tonsure them or kill them and then divide the kingdom of our brother, their father, between us." They sent Arcadius, a noble and able man, to the queen at Paris, saying sadly: "Say to our mother, that she should send to us the sons of our brother, our nephews, so that we might make them kings." Clotild, believing this to be true, rejoiced, and sent her grandsons to their uncles. Immediately, they sent Arcadius back to the queen saying: "These are scissors, and see here a sword. Thus tell your sons if you wish them to tonsure the boys or to kill them with the sword." Indeed, she was filled with a great deal of sadness and bitterness in her heart and with tears she said: "Enough, my narrow choice squeezes me from all sides. If they may not rule, for what reason did I raise them? It is better to be dead than to be tonsured." Then Arcadius brought back word falsely saying: "Thus the queen speaks, she prefers that they be killed rather than tonsured." Without delay, Chlotar grabbed hold of the older boy, threw him to the ground, and plunged his knife into his armpit. Having been run through, he died instantly. When his younger brother saw this, he threw himself at the feet of Childebert saying while crying: "Help me most pious father, so that I may not die like my brother did." Then Childebert moved to tears, said: "I ask you, most sweet brother, that by your kindness you order that his life be conceded to me, and whatsoever you might wish for this I will give to you." Burning with anger, Chlotar said: "Either you throw him away from you or surely you will die for him. It was you who brought about this evil counsel, and now do you wish to free him?" Hearing these things, Childebert threw him away from him. Chlotar dashed this one to the ground also, stabbed him under the armpit with his knife, killed him, just as he did his brother, and similarly he cut the throats of the boy's guards and servants. After this they mounted their horses, and Chlotar left. The queen heard of these doings. With very greatly deserved suffering she had their bodies prepared with many psalms and with immense lamentation she had the bodies which were carried to Paris buried. One of the children had been ten years of age and the other one had been seven. Indeed, a third one, Chlodovald, escaped, and through the help of strong-arm boys, he was freed. Afterward, Chlodovald gave up the kingdom of the world and tonsured himself by his own hand. He was made a cleric, he performed good works, and was ordained a priest. He went to the Lord full of virtue and rests buried at the villa of Novient, a suburb of Paris. Moreover, Queen Clotild lavishly distributed alms, spending her life in the highest degree of abstinence and sobriety.

§

25

[Concerning the death of Theuderic and the kingdom
of Theudebert and the war against Chlotar]

In these days King Theuderic died; he had reigned for
twenty-three years. Theudebert, his son, received his
kingdom. After this Childebert and Theudebert joined their
army together and made ready to campaign against Chlotar.
However, he heard of this, and seeing that he was not able to
resist their army, he fled into the forest of La Brotonne.
There he had constructed a breastwork and placed his entire
hope in God's piety. Queen Clotild, hearing about this, went
to the tomb of the blessed Martin, and there prostrated
herself in prayer, holding a vigil through the entire night,
praying that a civil war might not develop among her sons.
When they came together with large armies against Chlotar,
so that on the following day they would kill him, the dawn
broke in the place in which they were gathered and with the
sun up a furious storm with a mixture of lightning,
cloudbursts, and loud thunder blew away the tents and
overturned everything. Indeed, they prostrated themselves,
throwing themselves to the ground and they were severely
pelted with large hailstones. Nothing remained to cover them
except their shields, and they feared greatly that they would
be burned up by the heavenly fire. Their horses were so
scattered that they were scarcely recovered twenty stadia

away. Many of them were never found. While they were
pelted by hailstones and prostrate on the ground, they
repented and sought God's pardon for having wished to go
against one of their own blood. Over Chlotar's camp not a
drop of rain fell, no sound of thunder was heard nor was a
gust of wind felt. The brothers sent envoys seeking peace and
concord with Chlotar. After this was obtained, they returned
to their own lands.

§

26

[Childebert and Chlotar invaded Spain and besieged Saragossa.
The Lombards were made to pay tribute]

After this, Childebert and Chlotar again raised a large
army and invaded Spain. After having entered Spain they
devastated and burned the land and killed the people. They
encircled the city of Saragossa and besieged it. The people in
it who were kept blockaded put on hairshirts, sprinkled their
heads with ashes, were turned in great humility to God, and
carrying the cloak of the martyr, Saint Vincent, they walked
around the walls of the city singing psalms. The women,
similarly dressed in black cloaks, followed weeping with their
hair unbound as if the fast of Nineveh was being celebrated.
The kings, seeing these things, thought that some kind of evil
was being brought on them. Then they seized one of the
rustics from the countryside and asked him what it was that
they were doing. He said: "Lord, they are carrying the cloak
of the blessed martyr Vincent and with it they ask the Lord
to pity them." And the king said: "Go, tell the bishop of the
city, that he may come to us safely." The rustic, indeed,
announced this to the bishop. The latter hurriedly came with
gifts. Childebert requested that he should give him the relics
of the blessed Vincent. The bishop, however, gave his own
cloak to Childebert. Nevertheless, the already mentioned
kings conquered the greater part of Spain and returned home

with much booty. Childebert, indeed, coming to Paris, built a church in honor of the blessed martyr Vincent. Then King Theudebert, son of Theuderic, entered Italy with a large force. The Lombards were defeated and left prostrate. He devastated the greater part of the land and subjugated the Lombards as tributaries and returned home with a great deal of booty.

§

27

[Concerning the death of Theudebert, Clotild, and Theudebald. How Chlotar took his kingdom and the war against the Saxons]

After this Theudebert took ill and wracked by a high fever he died. He had reigned for fourteen years. Theudebald, his son, received in succession his Frankish kingdom in Austrasia. Thereafter, Queen Clotild of good memory and prepared with good works went to the Lord full of days at the city of Tours. With a great deal of psalm singing she was taken from Tours to Paris and in the holy church of Saint Peter at the side of King Clovis, her husband, she was buried by her sons. She was laid in the ground by the kings Childebert and Chlotar. There the blessed Geneviève is also buried. King Chlotar had by various women seven children. By Ingund, he had Gunthar, Childeric, Charibert, Guntram, Sigibert, and his daughter Chlothsind; by Charegunde, the sister of Ingund, he had Chilperic; and by Guntheuc he had Chramn. For love of Ingund, because she was beautiful and graceful, and because he was too luxury loving, he took her sister Charegunde in marriage. Moreover, in Austrasia, King Theudebald, the son of King Theudebert, came down with a high fever and died. He had reigned seven years. King Chlotar took over Theudebald's kingdom along with many treasures. In that year, the Saxons having rebelled, King Chlotar gathered an army of Franks and marched against them into battle on the Weser river. He struck down the greatest part of their army and devastated their land. He also went through all of Thuringia and depopulated it because the Thuringians had provided aid to the Saxons.

§

28

[How Chramn made a conspiracy against his father with
Childebert and concerning the death of Childebert]

So Chramn, the son of Chlotar, handsome and fit, but too
rough and violent, when he was sent by his father to a place
beyond the Loire, began to oppress the region with great
injustice. When this was made known to Chlotar, he ordered
him to come to him. But Chramn did not wish to obey his
father's order and continued acting in this hard manner. He
took as his wife a daughter of Willechar by the name of
Chalda. After having taken many treasures he came to Paris.
With King Childebert, his uncle, he was bound by an oath,
swearing to be the most constant enemy of his father. King
Childebert, however, began to take ill, he was felled for many
days with a fever at Paris and died. He was buried in the
church of the blessed martyr Vincent which he had
constructed. Chlotar took over his kingdom and treasures.
Chramn, also, was not able to go against his father and went
to Brittany. There with Conomor, king of the Bretons, he
and his wife and his children stayed hidden. Willechar, his
father-in-law, fled to the church of Saint Martin at Tours.
Then the church through the sins of Willechar and his wife
was burned. After which King Chlotar ordered it to be roofed
with tin and the inside also was restored to its former
splendor. After this King Chlotar gathered an army and

marched into Brittany to crush Chramn. But Chramn, not fearing to go to war against his father with his ally King Conomor of the Bretons, marched out. And when they fought against one another bravely, King Chlotar was moved to tears and said: "Look down from heaven, O Lord, and judge justly, and do as You did between Absalom and his father David." When the armies were joined in battle equally, the king of the Bretons turned in flight and there he fell. Chramn also tried to escape by flight, having prepared ships in the sea. But while he wished to free his wife and children, he was hemmed in by his father's army, captured, and tied up. When this was told to Chlotar, he ordered that Chramn with his wife and children be consumed by fire. Thus they were shut up in the hut of a poor man. Chramn was stretched out on a bench and strangled with a scarf. Then the little hut was burned up on top of him with his wife and children.

§

29

[What happened when Saint Medard died and concerning the death of Chlotar and how his sons succeeded to his kingdom]

Also in these times the most blessed bishop Medard, full of virtues, famous and glorious, went to the Lord. King Chlotar had him buried in the city of Soissons very gloriously and with a great deal of psalm singing. He also gave many gifts there. Indeed, King Chlotar went to the tomb of Saint Martin, prayed there for a long time, and distributed many gifts there, giving many gifts to the many churches of the saints. After this, while he exercised by hunting in the forest of Cuise, he was taken by a very high fever; from there he went to his villa at Compiègne. While there, when he was very gravely pained, he said: "Wa Wa! What do you think, what is this King of heaven like who kills thus such great kings?" In his weariness he gave up his spirit. He died in the fifty-first year of his reign. His four sons brought him in great honor to Soissons and buried him in the church of the blessed Medard. Chilperic, after his father's death, took treasures which were at the villa of Berny and sought out the most useful Franks and brought them to his support with many gifts. And soon he entered Paris and occupied the seat of King Childebert; but he was not permitted to hold it for long. For his brothers joined together and drove him out of there. Thus among these four, that is, Charibert, Guntram, Chilperic, and Sigibert, they arranged among themselves a legitimate division. Charibert took the kingdom of Childebert and established Paris as his seat; Guntram took the kingdom of Chlodomer, and set up his capital at Orléans; Chilperic taking the kingdom of his father Chlotar, established his seat at the city of Soissons; and Sigibert took the kingdom of Theuderic, setting up his seat in the city of Rheims.

§

30

[The Huns who invaded Gaul were defeated, the wars between Sigibert and Chilperic, and the wives of Charibert]

Therefore after the death of King Chlotar, the Huns having been on the move, with Cagano, their king, determined to come to Gaul. Sigibert moved his army against them and bravely battled them. He cut down the Huns with the sword, conquered them, and pursued them. But afterward their king sought friendship with Sigibert and through his envoys he asked for peace with him and returned to his own land. While, however, Sigibert was delayed, Chilperic, his brother collected an army and came through Rheims and devastated Champagne, burning and taking booty. Sigibert, returning the victor over the Huns, moved his army against Chilperic. He occupied the city of Soissons. There he found Theudebert, the son of Chilperic, captured him and sent him into exile. Moving, moreover, against Chilperic, he marched to war. Having defeated and forced Chilperic to flee, Sigibert once again restored his cities to his own lordship. Theudebert, Chilperic's son, Sigibert ordered to be kept under guard for a whole year at the villa of Pontion. Afterwards, because of his peaceful nature Sigibert returned Theudebert to his father safely. This was done, however, after Theudebert was made to swear an oath to Sigibert that he would never go against him again. Later, falling into sin, Theudebert went back on this oath. King Charibert led to wife Ingoberg. The queen had two servant girls who were the daughters of a poor man. The girls were very pretty and beautiful. The elder one was called Marcovefa and the younger was called by the name Merofled. King Charibert was excessively excited by love for these girls. Ingoberg hated them with great passion because of this and thus she ordered that their father become a wool worker. King Charibert was very much angered at this; he left Ingoberg and took Merofled to wife. After this he coupled in union with her sister, Marcovefa. For this reason both of them were excommunicated by Saint Germanus the bishop of Paris. But when the king did not wish to leave her, he was struck by the judgement of God and died.

§

31

[Concerning the death of Charibert, and how Sigibert took Brunhild to wife for himself and Chilperic took Galswintha and concerning Fredegund]

Not a long time after King Charibert died he was buried in the church of the holy Romanus in the fortress town of Blaye. When Sigibert saw that his brothers took unworthy wives for themselves and united in marriage with servant women, he sent a legation into Spain with many gifts and sought Brunhild, the daughter of King Athanagild. Athanagild did not reject Sigibert and he sent much treasure to him. He also received Brunhild with great preparation and immense joy as his wife. Because she had been under Arian law, Sigibert directed her to be baptized in the name of the Holy Trinity. King Chilperic seeing this, although he already had many wives, sought Brunhild's sister, Galswintha by name. He promised through his envoys to send away his other wives. Her father, indeed, hearing these promises, sent his daughter with many treasures to Chilperic. Galswintha was older than Brunhild. Truly, Chilperic took her in marriage with great joy and when she was baptized in the name of the Holy Trinity a good Christian was made. However, because Fredegund hated Galswintha, the former very wickedly created a scandal between the king and queen. Galswintha told the king that she was not able to bear such great injuries on account of her enemy Fredegund. She asked him to allow her to return freely to her father with the treasures remaining from those that she had brought with her from Spain. But he mollified her with tender words. After this, through the wicked counsel of Fredegund, he strangled Galswintha at night in her bed. After her death because of her merit a miracle was displayed by God. After that had been done, Chilperic's brothers were indignant about what had happened and wanted to eject him from his kingdom. At that time Chilperic had three sons by Audovera his queen; they were Theudebert, Merovech, and Clovis. Now, however, let us return to the beginning and learn how Fredegund deceived her lady Audovera, the queen. That same Fredegund was from a family of low rank. When King Chilperic went with his brother with an army against the Saxons, Audovera being pregnant remained at home. She gave birth to a daughter. Fredegund then by her cleverness gave counsel to her saying: "My lady, behold! my lord king is returning the victor; how can he receive his unbaptized daughter with rejoicing?" When the queen heard this, she ordered the baptismal font to be prepared and summoned the bishop who should baptize the daughter. When the bishop came, there was no lady present who should hold the girl. And Fredegund said: "We will never be able to find your equal to hold her. How excited she is, hold her." She therefore, hearing this, held her at the sacred font. Moreover, the victorious king having come, Fredegund went out to meet him, saying: "Praise God, because our lord king received victory over his enemies, and a daughter was born to you. With whom will my lord king sleep this night, because my lady, the queen is concerned with being a mother to your daughter Childasinda?" And he said: "If I cannot sleep with her, I will sleep with you." When the king entered his hall, the queen ran with her daughter to meet him, and the king said to her: "You did an abominable thing through your innocence;

indeed, you can no longer be my wife." He then asked her to dress in the habit of a nun along with her daughter. He gave her many estates and villas. Besides, he condemned the bishop who baptized the girl to exile. Then he made Fredegund his queen.

§

32

[The war between Sigibert and Chilperic and concerning the death of Sigibert]

At that time the Emperor Justinian died at the city of Constantinople; Justin took over the empire. Clovis, the younger son of Chilperic, went to the city of Bordeaux. While he remained there he bothered no one. Sigulf, however, a follower of Sigibert, having been sent with an army attacked him. Clovis fled, pursued with horns and trumpets like a fleeing deer. He barely escaped and reached his father at Paris. Chilperic also ordered his oldest son Theudebert who before had sworn an oath to Sigibert to lead a force beyond the Loire. Theudebert went to the cities of his uncle Sigibert, that is Tours, Poitiers, and the other ones. At Poitiers, moreover, he fought against Duke Gundoald; and Gundoald's army having been defeated he fled. Theudebert made a great slaughter of Gundoald's army. Then moving his army, he went to the Limousin and Cahors and he went through the region and devastated it. He burned many churches, and broke up many services, killed clergymen, destroyed the monasteries of men and his troops disported themselves at those of girls. They devastated everything. At this time there was worse lamenting in the churches than in the days of the persecutions of the emperors Maximianus and Diocletian. When these discords between the brothers seemed to spread,

Chilperic again moved his army against Rheims waging war and burning everything. Hearing about this, Sigibert brought together the peoples who lived on the other side of the Rhine, came to Paris and prepared to go against his brother. He sent messengers to the people of Chateaudun and of Tours so that they should go against Theudebert. When they neglected his order, the king sent the dukes Godegisel and Guntram to take over command. These dukes gathered the levies and had them go against Theudebert. He, however, was deserted by his followers and only a few of his men remained with him. But, nevertheless, he went to fight without wavering. They came together in battle, Theudebert was defeated decisively and was killed there. Duke Arnulf took his body and brought it to the city of Angoulême where it was buried. Chilperic fleeing through Rouen with his wife and children entered the city of Tournai, locked himself up there and prepared the defense. Sigibert took the cities which were on the other side of Paris up to Rouen. From there he returned to Paris, entered it, and there Brunhild and his children came to him. Then the Franks who had followed the elder Childebert sent a legation to Sigibert so that he might come to them and they having given up Chilperic would establish him above them as king. Hearing this, he sent a force to besiege his brother in the above-mentioned city of Tournai and he indicated that he would follow them with his army. Then the blessed Bishop Germanus said: "If you go out and you do not wish to kill your brother you will live and return the victor; but if you have thought to do otherwise you will most certainly die. For thus the Lord had spoken by the mouth of Solomon: 'If you prepare a pit for your brother you shall fall in it yourself.' " But the king neglected to listen. When he came to the villa named Vitry, the whole army gathered together around him and placing him upon a shield they established him as king over them. Then Fredegund got two armed thugs from the Thérouanne region, made them drunk and said to them: "Hear my counsel and go to Sigibert and feign to be his supporters so that you may raise the king up above you and kill him. If you escape alive, I will honor you and your children with wonderful things. If you perish there, I promise to give a great deal of alms in the places of the saints for you. They had no doubts since they were wild-hearted, and coming to Sigibert, making believe that they were going to support him, they drew their scramasaxes and stabbed him from both sides. He cried out and fell, giving up his spirit, and died. There also the murders fell. But Chilperic, not knowing that his brother was dead, feared all the following day to be captured by his brother's army. Only after Fredegund told him about what happened, that his brother was dead, did he stop fearing. Then Chilperic left Tournai with his wife and his followers. He buried Sigibert dressed in his most ornate clothes at the village of Lambres. Later they buried him in the church of the holy Medard at Soissons next to his father Chlotar. He died in the fourteenth year of his reign. After he died, Brunhild lived at Paris with her children full of grief and not knowing what she ought to do because of her sorrow. Duke Gundoald took Childebert, her young son, secretly at night and carried him away and fled with him to Austrasia. After having gathered together, the people over whom his father had reigned, set him up as king.

§

33

[How Brunhild was sent into exile and Merovech took her
as his wife and the war of the men of Champagne]

Indeed, King Chilperic came to Paris, seized Brunhild, and
put her in exile at the city of Rouen. He took possession of
the treasures which she had brought to Paris and ordered that
her daughter be held at the city of Meaux. Chilperic then sent
his son Merovech with an army beyond the Loire. But
Merovech, neglecting his father's orders, then returned
through Le Mans, on the pretext of visiting his mother
Audovera. He then came to the city of Rouen and there he
joined Queen Brunhild and married her. Evidently it was
against both the divine law and the laws of the canons for
Merovech to take in marriage the wife of his uncle. Thus
because of this Chilperic, upon hearing about what happened,
was very bitter and set out hurriedly for Rouen. Indeed,
when Merovech and Brunhild learned that Chilperic intended
to separate them, they fled to the church of Saint Martin
which is built of wooden planks upon the city walls. The king
was not able to get them out by tricks, so he swore
deceitfully to them that if it was God's will he would never
separate them. They, having heard these oaths, left the
church and he kissed them deceitfully and feasted with them.
A few days afterward, however, he returned to Soissons
taking Merovech with him. While they remained there a

group of men from Champagne gathered an army to go against Chilperic. He moved his army also and did battle. The levy of Champagne was soundly defeated and fled. Chilperic killed many very important men there. After these events, King Chilperic having been provoked by Fredegund began to suspect that Merovech because of his marriage to Brunhild was responsible for this evil, the raising of an army and the battle. Then he deprived Merovech of his arms and handed him over to guards so that they might control him. After this Chilperic had Merovech tonsured and ordered him to be ordained as a priest. When he had been dressed in the priestly habit, Chilperic ordered him to the monastery of Aninsola in Le Mans so that he might live according to the rule in that place. At that time the blessed Germanus, bishop of Paris, full of virtues, went to the Lord; he was buried in the church of the blessed Vincent with glory. After this, the younger Childebert sent a legation to Chilperic because of Brunhild, his mother. He asked that she be returned peacefully. Then Samson, Chilperic's son, died.

§

34

[Concerning the evil tax lists which Chilperic
ordered drawn up]

Moreover, at the counsel of Fredegund, King Chilperic
ordered new and very heavy tax assessments drawn up for his
entire realm. Because of this many left the land, the villas,
the cities, and their private possessions, seeking another
kingdom. They said that it is better to migrate than to be
subjected to such danger. For it was enacted that each owner
of private property should pay one amphora of wine for each
arpent of land. They also imposed this tax on the remainder
of land tenures and on everything of value including slaves.
The people, indeed, were greatly oppressed and cried out
aloud to the Lord. At that time Chilperic was gravely ill.
After he recovered, his youngest son, not yet baptized, began
to take ill. After he was baptized he just barely recovered and
then his older brother, Chlodobert, was taken by the disease
and wasted away greatly. Fredegund, filled with her sons'
pain and with a groan, said to the king, repenting: "The
divine mercy has for a long time tolerated our evil deeds for
we have had fevers and other sicknesses but we have never
mended our ways. Behold, now we lose our sons; behold,
now they are killed by the tears of the poor, by the groans of
the widows, and by the sighs of orphans! Behold the great
weights of gold and silver, the storerooms and the wine

cellars overflow, and we do not know for what reason we collect it. Behold, we have lost the most handsome boy that we had. How will all this turn out for us? Now, indeed, let my counsel please you, and order to be given back that which we took in excess and order that the new unfair tax lists which we made up unjustly be burned so that if we have indeed lost the children at least we will escape perpetual punishment." Then the king, with compunction in his heart, handed over all of the unfair tax lists to be burned in the fire. After this the young boy, his son, died. With great grief they carried him to the church of the martyr Saint Denis at Paris and buried him. Then Chlodobert, their other son, was taken very ill, and they put him on a litter and took him to the church of the holy Medard at Soissons. They placed him by the holy tomb and made vows for him; but he weakened during the night and died. They buried him in the church of the holy martyrs Crispin and Crispinian. A great noise was raised by all the people for women with their husbands bewailed sorrowfully dressed in black clothes and followed the funeral beating their breasts. King Chilperic gave many presents and gifts to the churches and to the poor and many villas were distributed.

§

35

[Concerning the Emperors Justin and Tiberius and the subjugation of Italy. The death of King Guntram and how Chilperic was killed through the cleverness of Fredegund]

In that year the Emperor Justin who had gone mad died in the city of Constantinople during the eighteenth year of his reign. Tiberius succeeded to his power. After this the boy Theuderic, the son of Chilperic, died. Also in these days, Fredegund gave birth to another son whom they called Chlotar. After this he went on to become a great king and was the father of Dagobert. And so Childebert the king of Austrasia went with his army into Italy; he devastated it and made it tributary. Also in those days great quarrels arose between Chilperic and Childebert his nephew. Indeed, Fredegund and Brunhild incited them on both sides. Also at that time the lord king Guntram of good memory, brother of King Chilperic, died. He was buried in Chalons, a city in Burgundy, in the church of the martyr Saint Marcellus. Guntram had ruled for thirty-one years. Then Fredegund sent her daughter Rigunth to King Leuvogild to be the wife of his son. She sent with her many treasures and great wealth with a large escort of Goths. Queen Fredegund, moreover, was beautiful and very clever and also an adulteress. At that time Landeric was the mayor of the palace. He was a clever and able man whom the above-mentioned queen loved very much because he was joined with her in wanton living. One day very early in the morning the king went out to exercise at hunting at the villa of Chelles near Paris. Since he loved Fredegund too much, he returned from the horse stable to the palace bedroom. Fredegund was in the bedroom washing her hair with her head in the water. The king came up behind her and whacked her on the buttocks with a stick. She, thinking that it was Landeric, said: "Why do you do this, Landeric?" Then she looked up and behind her and saw that it was the king; she was very scared. The king, indeed, was very much saddened and went off to his hunt. Fredegund then called Landeric to her and told him all these things that the king had done and seen, saying: "Plan what you should do, because tomorrow we will be subjected to a great deal of torture." And Landeric, with his resolve weakened and moved to tears, said: "My eyes saw you at a bad time. I do not know what I should do because problems close in on me from all sides." She said to him: "Do not fear. Hear my counsel and let us do this and we will not die. When the day ends, the king will have returned at night from hunting. Let us send someone who will kill him and who will shout that Childebert the treacherous king of Austrasia did it. And when the king has been killed, we will rule with my son Chlotar." When night came, King Chilperic returned from the hunt. While he was dismounting from his horse and those of his party were returning to their homes, the assassins, sent by Fredegund and drunk on her wine, swordsmen to be sure, stabbed the king in the belly with two scramasaxes. Chilperic cried out and died. The murderers whom the queen had sent clamored: "Ambush, ambush, this is what King Childebert of Austrasia did to our lord." Then Chilperic's guards ran here and there. When they found nothing, they returned to their homes. Thereupon, Mallulf, the bishop of Senlis, who was present at that time in the palace, dressed Chilperic in his royal robes and had him taken to Paris with Queen

Fredegund and the remainder of his armed followers. He was taken into the nave of the church of the holy martyr Vincent with hymns and psalm singing and buried there. He had reigned for twenty-three years. Fredegund, however, with the young king Chlotar and with Landeric whom they chose as mayor of the palace, remained in the kingdom. Also, the Franks established the before-mentioned young king Chlotar over them in the kingdom.

§

36

[Fredegund went to war with the Austrasians, defeated them
and burned Champagne]

After King Childebert of Austrasia, the son of Sigibert
and the nephew of Chilperic, heard of the death of his uncle
and the wicked deeds of Queen Fredegund, he gathered an
army. For with the death of Guntram, his uncle, he had
received the kingdom of Burgundy. The Burgundians, the
Austrasians, and the Frankish magnates gathered an army
together, they departed quickly for Champagne, entered into
the district of Soissons, and devastated it under the
leadership of the patricians Gundoald and Wintrio. When
Fredegund heard this she gathered an army with Landeric
and the other Frankish dukes. Having come to the villa of
Berny Rivière, she enriched the Franks with many gifts and
presents and mobilized them to fight against their enemies.
When she indicated that all too soon a reinforced army of
Austrasians would be there, she gave counsel to the Franks
who were with her, saying: "Let us go against them at night
with lights carried by our retainers who will go in front of us
with branches of trees in their hands and little bells tied on
their horses so that the enemy's watchful guards cannot
recognize us. With the dawn at the beginning of day, we will
go against them and perhaps we will defeat them
completely." This counsel was accepted. When the plan had

been made they agreed on which day they should come together for battle in the place called Droisy in the district of Soissons. Just as she had advised, they started at night with their arms readied and with branches in the hands of those others concerning whom we spoke above. Mounted on their horses and with the young king Chlotar being carried in their arms, they came as far as Droisy. When, however, the guards of the Austrasian army saw the tree branches in masses in front of the Frankish line and when the guards heard the ringing of the bells, one man said to his companion: "Yesterday was there not a field there and also in that place, how is it then that we see a forest there now?" His companion said, laughing: "But of course you have been drunk, that is how you blotted it out. Do you not hear the bells of our horses grazing next to that forest?" After all this happened and the dawn of day was breaking, the Franks charged in over the sleeping Austrasians and Burgundians with a blast of trumpets. And with Fredegund and young Chlotar they killed the largest part of that army, a countless number, a very large force, from the highest to the lowest. Gundoald and also Wintrio slipped away by flight, they barely escaped. Landeric, in fact, pursued Wintrio, who with the aid of his very fast horse escaped. Fredegund, indeed, with the rest of the army went as far as Rheims. She set fire to Champagne and devastated it. Then she returned home with much booty and many spoils.

§

37

[Concerning the death of Fredegund and the wars between Theudebert and Chlotar]

At that time Childebert, king of Austrasia, had two sons; the older, who was named Theudebert, he had by a concubine; the younger, who was named Theuderic, he had by the queen. Theudebert himself sent his grandmother Brunhild into Burgundy, the kingdom of the great king Guntram. Moreover, at that time Queen Fredegund, old and full of days, died. She was buried in the basilica of Saint Vincent the martyr at Paris. Theuderic, the king of Burgundy, was handsome and energetic and very hot-headed. With the counsel of his grandmother Brunhild he gathered a very large army from Burgundy and led it against Chlotar, his cousin. Chlotar, upon hearing about this, mobilized the army of the Franks and went against Theuderic hurriedly. The two armies met each other in the district of Sens on the banks of the River Orvanne, they charged against each other in battle. So many people were killed in that place that the river was filled with bodies of the dead and the water was not able to flow because of the accumulated gore. In that battle there was an angel of the Lord with an unsheathed sword over the people. King Chlotar, seeing his defeated army dispersed in flight, entered Melun, a fortified place on the river Seine; afterward he went to Paris. Theuderic, in fact, having devastated that region and also burning as far as the village of Essone, returned home with much booty.

§

38

[Concerning Brunhild's evil counsel and how
Theuderic killed his brother]

Chlotar left Paris and entered the forest of La Brotonne.
Brunhild, moreover, daily supplied Theuderic with evil
counsel saying: "Why do you neglect and why do you not
demand your father's treasure and his kingdom from the
hand of Theudebert since you know that he is not your
brother because he was conceived in adultery with a
concubine of your father?" When Theuderic heard this and
since he was fierce at heart, he mobilized a large army and
directed it against his brother Theudebert. They marched out
to battle at Zülpich, a fortified place. After they fought
bravely, Theudebert, seeing that his army was defeated,
turned in flight and entered the city of Cologne. Theuderic,
therefore, having burned and devastated the land of the
Ripuarians, that people handed themselves over into his hands,
saying: "Stop lord king, we and our land are already yours,
do not further destroy our people." And he said: "Either
bring me Theudebert alive or bring me his severed head if you
want me to spare you." They then entered Cologne, some
lying on the behalf of others, said to Theudebert: "Your
brother commands you, 'Give up your father's treasure which
you have with you and thus afterwards he will withdraw with
his people.' " And when the liars said these things to him, he
went with them into the palace for his treasure. When he
asked for the open boxes of treasures and ornaments, one of
the men having drawn his sword struck Theudebert from

behind in the neck. After, they took his head and held it up on the wall of the city of Cologne. Thus, Theuderic seeing this, occupied that city, taking a great deal of treasure. Afterwards the Frankish magnates swore oaths to him in the church of the martyr Saint Gereonus. It seemed to Theuderic that he had been struck craftily in secret, and he said: "Watch the enemy; I do not know which of those lying Ripuarians struck me." And when they unwound his clothes, they did not find anything except a small purple mark. From there, indeed, he returned home with many spoils including the sons and beautiful daughter of his brother, King Theudebert. Theuderic returned to the city of Metz and Queen Brunhild came to him there. Having seized the boys, he killed the sons of Theudebert. Indeed, he dashed out the brains of the youngest, who was still in the white of baptism, by striking him against a stone.

§

39

[Theuderic wished to take his niece in marriage
and how Theuderic was killed by Brunhild]

When Theuderic saw Theudebert's beautiful daughter, his
own niece, he wished to join with her in marriage. Brunhild
said to him: "How can you take the daughter of your
brother?" And he answered: "Did you not tell me that he
was not my brother? Why have you made me sin so that I
have killed my brother? Evil woman!" And unsheathing his
sword, he wished to kill her. She, in fact, was pulled away by
the noblemen who were standing around, and she barely
escaped by slipping into the bedroom of the house. Thus she
hated him very much and slipped him a poisonous potion by
the hand of wicked agents. King Theuderic was ignorant of
this and drank the potion. He grew weak and his impious
spirit was diminished by his sins. He died. Brunhild then
killed his young sons.

§

40

[How the Austrasians and the rest of the Franks raised Chlotar up as king and condemned Brunhild to death]

After these kings died, the Burgundians and the Austrasians made peace with the rest of the Franks, and raised up King Chlotar to the kingship over all three kingdoms. So King Chlotar, having mobilized an army, sent it into Burgundy to Brunhild feigning as though he would join her in alliance. He asked her to come to him as if for peace. She, in fact, adorned in the royal dress, came to him at the fortified place on the river Tiron. When he saw her he said: "O enemy of the Lord, why have you done so much evil and dared to kill so many of the royal line?" Then the army of the Franks and Burgundians joined into one, all shouted together that death would be most fitting for the very wicked Brunhild. Then King Chlotar ordered that she be lifted on to a camel and led around through the entire army. Then she was tied to the feet of wild horses and torn apart limb from limb. Finally she died. Her final grave was the fire. Her bones were burnt. The king, in fact, having made peace all around, returned home. The noble Gundoald, the mayor of the palace at the king's court, was an outstanding and diligent man.

§

41

[Where the Saxons did battle against Dagobert and Chlotar
killed their duke and did not spare any man of them
who was taller than his sword]

Then there was King Chlotar's son who was named
Dagobert. He was a capable boy and also energetic and clever
in all things and very accomplished. The king sent him when
he was a young man with Peppin, the duke in Austrasia, so
that he might learn to rule. The Austrasians, indeed, the
leading Franks gathered in a group and established Dagobert
over them as king. Also in those days the very rebellious
Saxons moved an army of many peoples against King
Dagobert and Chlotar. Dagobert gathered a large force,
crossed the Rhine, and did not hesitate to march out to
battle against the Saxons. While these forces were fighting
against each other fiercely, Dagobert was struck on the
helmet which was on his head, a part of his hair was cut off
and fell to the ground. His armor bearer, standing behind
him, picked it up. Dagobert seeing his people defeated said to
his follower: "Go quickly, hurry with the hair from my head
to my father so that he may come quickly to us before the
entire army is conquered." He traveled rapidly, crossed the
Ardennes forest, and went as far as the [Rhine] river. King
Chlotar came there with a large army. When the messenger
came hurriedly, carrying the hair which had been cut from

Dagobert's head to the king, Chlotar was grief-stricken. With the sound of trumpets, starting at night, he crossed over the Rhine with his army and hurriedly came to the aid of his son. When they were united together they clapped their hands with cheerful hearts. They pitched their tents and camped beside the Weser river. Bertoald, the duke of the Saxons, standing on the other side of the river prepared to fix a time so that he might go out to fight. Upon hearing the uproar of the people, he asked what this was all about. They replied, saying: "The lord king Chlotar has come and therefore the Franks are relieved." He replied with laughter, saying: "You liars, you are terrified of being wiped out when you say that Chlotar has come to you when we have heard that he is dead." The king was also standing there dressed up in his coat of mail, a helmet over the hair of his head, and wrapped in a cloak of dog skins. When the king took off his helmet and uncovered his head, Bertoald recognized that he was the king and said: "Is that you here, lying beast of burden?" The king, indeed, upon hearing this was very angry at this outburst and entered the Weser river on his fastest horse and swam across. Wild in his heart, he pursued Bertoald. The army of the Franks followed the king, swimming after him. With difficulty they crossed the river with Dagobert through the deep whirlpools. So King Chlotar pursued Bertoald and fought fiercely against him. And Bertoald said: "Withdraw from me, O King, or else I will kill you. Because if you manage to prevail against me, so all men will say that you killed your kinsman and servant Bertoald. If, however, I kill you, then a great rumor will be heard among all the peoples that the bravest king of the Franks was killed by a servant." The king, however, was by no means satisfied with what he said, but charged at him once again. Also the king's horsemen, having followed the king from a distance, shouted: "Be strong against your enemy, my lord king." The king's arm, however, became very heavy because he wore a coat of mail. Nevertheless the king charged at Bertoald again, killed him, and help up his head on his spear. Then he returned to the Franks. Those who did not know that the king was safe were sad until they saw him and rejoiced with great happiness. The king, indeed, devastated the entire land of the Saxons and killed their people. He did not leave alive there any man who stood taller than his sword which is called a long sword. He established this as a symbol in that region and returned as the victor to his own land.

§

42

[Concerning the death of Chlotar and the kingdom of Dagobert]

Indeed, time having passed, Chlotar the old king died. He had reigned for forty-four years. King Dagobert, his son, took the kingship in all three of his kingdoms. King Dagobert was very brave, the sustenance of the Franks, very strict in judgements, and the supporter of the churches. Indeed, he first ordered that much wealth from the royal fisc be distributed as alms through the churches of the saints. He established peace through all his kingdom. His reputation resounded among many peoples. He inspired fear and dread in all the kingdoms around. A peaceful man, just like Solomon, he maintained peace in the kingdom of the Franks. Then the blessed Bishop Audoin appeared on the scene. At this time Gundoald, the famous mayor of the palace, died. King Dagobert made the illustrious man Erchinoald mayor of the palace. The above-mentioned king had by his queen Nantchildis, who was a Saxon, two sons, Sigibert and Clovis. Sigibert, indeed, his elder son, he had established in the kingdom of Austrasia with Duke Peppin to direct things. Clovis the younger son he kept with him.

§

43

[Concerning the death of Dagobert and Sigibert and the kingdom of Clovis]

After this King Dagobert was seized by a high fever and wasting away, he died at Epinay-sur-Seine in the district of the city of Paris, and was buried in the church of the blessed martyr Saint Denis. The Franks lamented with a great deal of noise for many days. He had ruled for forty-four years. The Franks raised above them as king his son, Clovis; and he took as a wife a Saxon girl by the name of Balthildis. She was beautiful, clever, and of strong character. After this, however, King Sigibert of Austrasia died and Peppin who also died was replaced as mayor of the palace by his son Grimoald. Just after Sigibert died, Grimoald had the king's young son who was named Dagobert tonsured and directed Didon, the bishop of the city of Poitiers, to take the boy on a pilgrimage to Ireland. Then Grimoald placed his own son on the throne. The Franks were very indignant about this and they prepared an ambush for Grimoald. They seized him, and sent him to Clovis, king of the Franks, to be condemned. In the city of Paris he was put in prison, tightly bound with the torture of chains since he was worthy of dying as one who had harmed his lord. His death came with a great deal of torture.

§

44

[Concerning who ruined the kingdom of the Franks and the death of Clovis and the kingdom of Chlotar]

At this time, Clovis, having been instigated by the devil, cut off the arm of the blessed martyr Denis. At the same time he brought ruin to the kingdom of the Franks with disastrous calamities. This Clovis, moreover, had every kind of filthy habit. He was a seducer and a debaser of women, a glutton and a drunk. About his death and end nothing of historical worth may be said. Many writers condemn his end because they do not know the extent of his evil. Thus in uncertainty concerning it they refer from one to another. From Bathildis, his queen, three sons were born to him: Chlotar, Childeric, and Theuderic. And so time passing the above-mentioned King Clovis died. He had reigned for sixteen years. Indeed, the Franks established Chlotar, the eldest of the three boys, to be king in his place, with the queen-mother as regent.

§

45

[Ebroin was chosen as mayor of the palace, King Chlotar
died, and Theuderic and Childeric were established
in the kingdom]

At this time, the mayor Erchinoald having died, the
Franks vacillating in uncertainty, decided in council to
establish Ebroin in the high honor of mayor of the palace in
the king's court. In these days the boy king Chlotar died. He
had reigned for four years. Theuderic, his brother, was raised
up as king of the Franks. And so they had Childeric, his
brother, established in Austrasia with Duke Wulfoald as his
protector. At this time the Franks hostile to Ebroin prepared
an ambush. They rose up against Theuderic and deposed him.
Dragging them off by force, they tonsured Ebroin and sent
him to the monastery of Luxeuil in Burgundy. They agreed
and sent to nearby Austrasia for Childeric. He came with
Duke Wulfoald and was raised up over the kingdom of the
Franks. But this Childeric was much too frivolous and went
about everything much too carelessly. He stirred up a great
deal of hate and scandal by oppressing the Franks greatly.
One of these, a Frank by the name of Bodilo, he ordered tied
to a stake and severely beaten without legal cause. The
Franks seeing this were roused to great anger. Ingobert to be
sure, Amalbert, and other Frankish magnates stirred up an
insurrection against Childeric. Bodilo together with others

gathered to ambush the king. They killed him, and I am sorry to say that they killed his pregnant queen also. Wulfoald barely escaped by fleeing and returned to Austrasia. The Franks, moreover, chose Leudesius, the son of Erchinoald, as mayor of the palace. And from Burgundy the blessed Leudegar, bishop of Autun, and Gaerinus, his brother, agreed in this counsel. Ebroin, having let his hair grow back, gathered his followers to help him, left the monastery of Luxeuil in military array, and returned to Francia with their arms prepared. Indeed, Ebroin sent off a message to the blessed Audoin so that the holy man might give him counsel. But Audoin only sent messengers with a written message to Ebroin, saying: "May the memory of Fredegund help you." Ebroin understood because he was a clever man. Rising up during the night, the army moved and came up to the Oise River. After the guards had been killed there, he crossed the Oise at Pont-Sainte-Maxence. Those men whom he found in ambush he killed. Leudesius escaped along with King Theuderic and as many followers as could by flight. Ebroin followed them. Coming to the villa of Baizieux, Ebroin seized the royal treasure. Then after this he came to Crécy-en-Ponthieu where he recovered the king. As a trick Ebroin swore oaths promising Leudesius safety and summoned him to his presence. When Leudesius came, Ebroin killed him. He then cleverly recovered the mayorship. He ordered the holy bishop Leudegar to be killed with the sword after suffering various tortures; Gaerin, Leudegar's brother, Ebroin condemned with horrible tortures. Indeed, many surviving Franks who were their supporters barely escaped through flight. Some who fled into exile were deprived of their own private holdings.

§

46

[Duke Martin and Duke Peppin go to war against
Ebroin and Theuderic]

In that time also, Wulfoald having died in Austrasia,
Martin and Peppin the younger, son of the late Ansegisel,
were dominant in Austrasia because the kings had passed
from the scene. Then after some time had passed, these dukes
turned in hatred against Ebroin, gathered a large army of
Austrasians and directed their force against King Theuderic
and Ebroin. Ebroin and Theuderic with their army went
against the dukes. In a place called Bois-Royal du Fays the
armies joined together in battle and cut each other to pieces
with a great deal of slaughter. A countless number of people
fell there. The Austrasians, having been defeated, turned their
backs and slipped away in flight. Ebroin followed, cutting
them down very cruelly. He devastated the greater part of the
region. Martin escaped by flight, entered Laon, and shut
himself up in the place. Peppin, on the other hand, escaped.
Ebroin, having achieved victory, returned. Coming with his
army to the villa at Ecry, he sent envoys to Martin so that
after oaths had been taken in good faith the latter might
come to King Theuderic. Ebroin swore his oaths to Martin
deceitfully and falsely on empty boxes. But Martin believing
the oaths came to Ecry; there with his followers he was
killed.

§

47

[Ebroin was killed, Waratto was made mayor of the palace
and the blessed Audoin went to the Lord]

Thus it was that Ebroin oppressed the Franks more and
more cruelly. Then after some time a Frank named
Ermenfred secretly prepared a plot. At night Ermenfred
secretly rose up against him and cruelly killed the
above-mentioned Ebroin and escaped by fleeing to Peppin in
Austrasia. The Franks, after taking counsel, set up Waratto,
an illustrious man, in his place as mayor of the palace by
order of the king. Waratto received hostages among other
things from the aforementioned Peppin and made peace with
him. At this time, however, Waratto's son, an able and
diligent man by the name of Ghislemar, who had a wild spirit
and immature habits, ambushed his father. He cast his father
down from his very high honor and replaced him. The blessed
bishop Audoin prohibited him so that he might not carry out
this evil plot against his father, but Ghislemar refused to
listen. There was then much civil war between this Ghislemar
and Peppin. Ghislemar either because of the injuries that he
had inflicted upon his father or for other cruel sins was
struck down by God and breathed out his most iniquitous
spirit just as the blessed Audoin had predicted to him. After
Ghislemar died, Waratto again obtained his former honor. In
these days the blessed Audoin, bishop of Rouen, full of days

and remarkable virtues went to the Lord at the royal villa of Saint-Ouen-sur-Seine in the suburbs of the city of Paris. He was buried with glory in the church of the apostle Saint Peter in the city of Rouen.

§

48

[Waratto died and Berchar was established in his place.
Peppin defeated him and took into his control
the mayorship of the palace]

Indeed, following the passage of time, the above-mentioned Waratto died. He had a noble and talented wife by the name of Anseflidis. The Franks, to be sure, vacillated in various directions. Meanwhile the Franks, divided among themselves, set up Berchar in the position of mayor of the palace. He was puny in stature, ignoble in wisdom, and useless in counsel. Peppin rose up in Austrasia, gathered a rather large force, and led his array against King Theuderic and Berchar. They came together in battle in a place called Tetry and while they fought against each other, King Theuderic along with Berchar, the mayor of the palace, turned their backs. Peppin, indeed, emerged the victor. Shortly after this, Berchar was killed by some time-servers. At the instigation of Anseflidis, Peppin began to be mayor of the palace, the chief ruling agent of King Theuderic. Then Peppin took the treasure and returned to Austrasia. He left Nordebert, one of his followers, with the king. And Prince Peppin had a very noble and wise wife by the name of Plectrude. By her he begot two sons; the name of the elder was Drogo, the name, indeed, of the younger was Grimoald. Drogo received the dukedom of Champagne.

§

49

[Concerning the death of Theuderic, the kingdom of Clovis
and Childebert, and the mayor of the palace Grimoald]

King Theuderic died; he had reigned for nineteen years.
Clovis, his son, the boy having been born to the queen named
Chrodchild, took the royal seat. Not long afterward, the boy
king Clovis died; he had reigned for two years. Childebert, his
brother, a famous man, was established in the kingdom. Then
Nordebert died. Grimoald, the younger son of Prince Peppin,
was made mayor of the palace at the court of King
Childebert. Peppin also carried on many wars against the
pagan Radbod, against other princes, against the Sueves, and
against many other peoples as well. Grimoald, indeed, had a
son by the name of Theudoald by a concubine. In the course
of time Drogo, son of Peppin died. Peppin, the
above-mentioned prince, had by another wife named
[Alpaida] a son by the name of Charles. He was a graceful,
distinguished, and able man.

§

50

[Concerning the death of Childebert and the kingdom of
Dagobert. Because Grimoald was killed and in honor of
his father Theudoald was made mayor]

Then the most glorious lord Childebert, a just king of
good memory went to the Lord; he had reigned for seventeen
years and was buried at the monastery of Choisy-au-Bac in
the church of the protomartyr Saint Stephen. And Dagobert
a young boy, his son, reigned for him. Grimoald had taken a
wife in marriage by the name of Theudesinda, the daughter
of the pagan Duke Radbod. And this Grimoald, the mayor of
the palace, was pious, modest, mild, and just. After some
time, however, Prince Peppin became ill and when Grimoald
came to visit him without delay, he was murdered in the
church of the holy martyr Landebert in Liège by a pagan
named Rantgar, a son of Belial. Indeed, they established
Theudoald by the order of his grandfather in the high
honored seat of his father in the king's court.

§

51

[Concerning the death of Peppin, the civil wars of the Franks,
the flight of Theudoald, and the elevation of Ragamfred
to the chief office of the kingdom]

At this time Peppin was struck down by a high fever and died. He had held the chief position under the above-mentioned king for twenty-seven and one half years. Plectrude governed everything discreetly with her grandchildren and with the king. In these days, having been instigated by the devil, Franks again attacked Franks in the forest of Compiègne and killed each other most horribly. Theudoald, moreover, slipped away in flight, he crept away, and was at that time hotly pursued. Theudoald having fled, the Franks picked Ragamfred to be the chief officer, the mayor of the palace. Ragamfred, having gathered an army with the king, crossed the Charbonnière forest and devastated the lands up to the Meuse river. Then he became friends with the pagan duke Radbod. Charles, in these days, was held under guard by the lady Plectrude. With God's help, he escaped with difficulty.

§

52

[Concerning the death of Dagobert, the kingdom of
Chilperic, and how Charles waged war against Radbod]

With the passage of time, King Dagobert took sick and
died. He had reigned for five years. A one-time cleric named
Daniel whose hair had grown back on his head was
established in the kingdom by the Franks, and they called
him Chilperic. And to be sure, a short time later, they again
moved an army up to the Meuse river and directed it against
Charles. From the other side, the Frisians came under their
duke Radbod. Charles attacked the Frisians, and there were
great losses suffered by his followers. He slipped away in
flight and departed. With the passing of time, Chilperic with
Ragamfred, gathered an army, entered the Ardennes forest,
moved up to the Rhine river and penetrated the district of
Cologne where they devastated the land. After they received
a great deal of treasure from the lady Plectrude they
withdrew. But at a place called Amblève, Charles attacked
them, and they suffered extensive losses.

§

53

[Charles carried the battle against Chilperic and Ragemfred; in a place called Vinchy they were defeated and then they fled and Charles held the entire kingdom of the Franks in his power]

At that time the above-mentioned man Charles, having gathered an army, again went against Chilperic and Ragamfred. They also gathered an army and hurriedly prepared for war against him. But Charles asked that peace be made. They refused, and the two forces did battle in a place called Vinchy, on Sunday at dawn on the twenty-first day of March in Lent. After they fought against each other bravely, Chilperic with Ragamfred turned his back. Charles emerged the victor. After, Charles devastated many regions and took many captives. He returned to Austrasia with a great deal of booty. Upon coming to the city of Cologne, he instigated a revolt there. He discussed matters with the lady Plectrude, cleverly took back his father's treasure, and set up for himself a king by the name of Chlotar. And so Chilperic and Ragamfred sought out Duke Eudo for help. Eudo mobilized his army and went against Charles vigorously. But the intrepid Charles resolutely moved to attack him. Eudo fled and returned to the city of Paris. He then retreated with Chilperic and with the royal treasure and carried them across the Loire. Charles followed him but did not catch him.

Chlotar, the already mentioned king, died in that year, and Charles, the following year, sent a legation to Eudo and made friends with him. Indeed, Eudo returned King Chilperic along with many gifts, but he did not remain on the throne for long. He died after this and was buried in the city of Noyon. He had reigned for five and one half years. The Franks set up above themselves as king Theuderic who had been raised in the monastery of Chelles. He was a son of Dagobert the younger, and is now in the sixth year of his reign.

§

The *LHF* in Latin

3. Igitur post transactos decim annos misit memoratus imperator exactores una cum Primario duce de Romano senatu, ut darent consueta tributa de populo Francorum. Illi quoque, sicut erant crudeles et inmanissimi, consilio inutile accepto, dixerunt ad invicem: "Imperator cum exercitu Romano non potuit eicere Alanos d latibulis paludarum, gentem fortem ac rebellem; nos enim, qui eos superavimus, quur solvimus tributa? Consurgamus igitur contra Primarium hunc vel exactoribus istis percutiamusque eos et auferamus cuncta quae secum habent et non demus Romanis tributa et erimus non iugiter liberi". Insidiis vero praeparatis, interficerunt eos.

(This sample of the Latin of the *LHF* is drawn from chapter 3. The translation is to be found on page 25.)

Select Bibliography of Works available in English*

(*See also the works cited in the Introduction)

Bachrach, Bernard S. "Charles Martel, Mounted Shock Combat, the Stirrup, and Feudalism," *Studies in Medieval and Renaissance History*, VII (1970), 49-75.

————. "Procopius, Agathias, and the Frankish Military," *Speculum*, XLV (1970), 435-441.

————. "Procopius and the Chronology of Clovis' Reign," *Viator*, I (1970), 21-31.

————. *Merovingian Military Organization 481-751* (Minneapolis, 1972).

————. *Gregory of Tours, "History" Bk. vii* (Lawrence, Kan., 1972).

————. *A History of the Alans in the West* (Minneapolis, 1973).

————. "Was the Marchfield a part of the Frankish Constitution?" *Mediaeval Studies* (forthcoming).

Cameron, Averil, "How Did the Merovingian Kings Wear Their Hair?" *RBPH*, XLIII (1965), 1203-1216.

————. "Agathias on the Early Merovingians," *Annali della Scuola Normale Superiore di Pisa*, XXXVII (1968), 95-140.

Thompson, E. A. *The Early Germans* (Oxford, 1965).

Wallace-Hadrill, J. M. *The Barbarian West* (London, 1962).

————. *The Long-Haired Kings and Other Studies in Frankish History* (London, 1962).

————. "Gregory of Tours and Bede: Their Views on the Personal Qualities of Kings," *Frümittelalterlich Studien*, II (1968), 31-44.

Index

- 119 -

Merovingian Gaul

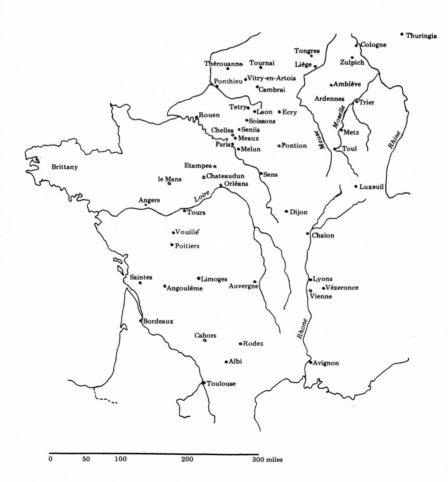

Thuringia

Cologne
Tongres
Liège
Zulpich
Thérouanne
Tournai
Amblève
Ponthieu
Vitry-en-Artois
Cambrai
Ardennes
Trier
Tetry
Laon
Ecry
Rouen
Soissons
Moselle
Chelles
Seniis
Metz
Meaux
Paris
Pontion
Toul
Melun
Rhine
Meuse
Etampes
le Mans
Chateaudun
Sens
Orléans
Luxeuil
Angers
Loire
Tours
Dijon
Vouillé
Chalon
Poitiers
Saintes
Limoges
Lyons
Angoulême
Auvergne
Vézeronce
Vienne
Bordeaux
Rhone
Cahors
Rodez
Albi
Avignon
Toulouse
Brittany

| 0 | 50 | 100 | 200 | 300 miles |

The Merovingian Genealogy as seen in the *Liber*

```
Priam                          Antenor
Marchomir                      Sunno
Faramund
Chlodio
Merovech
Childeric I
m. Basina
```

Clovis I — Landechildis — Albofledis
m. 1. ?
2. Clotild

1.	2.	2.	2.	2.	2.
Theuderic I	Ingomir	Chlodomer I m. Guntheuc	Childebert I	Chlotar I m.1. Ingund 2. Charegunde 3. Guntheuc	Chrodchild m. Amalaric
Theudebert I					
Theudebald I		Theudovald Chlodovald			

1.	1.	1.	1.	1.	2.	3.
Gunthar	Childeric	Charibert I m. Ingoberg Merofled Marcovefa	Guntram I	Sigibert I m. Brunhild	Chilperic I m.1. Audovera 2. Galaswintha 3. Fredegund	Chramn m. Chalda
				Childebert II		

Theudebert II   Theuderic II

1.	1.	1.	1.
Theudebert	Merovech m. Brunhild	Clovis	Childasinda

3.	3.	3.	3.	3.
Samson	Chlodobert	Theuderic	Chlotar II	Rigunth
			Dagobert I m. Nantchildis	

Clovis II   Sigibert III
m. Balthildis

Dagobert II

Chlotar III	Childeric II	Theudebert III m. Chrodchild
	Chilperic II	

Chlotar IV

Clovis III   Childebert III

Dagobert III

Theuderic IV

DATE DUE			